AN ANTHOLOGY OF

*SOMALI POETRY*_____

Translated by B.W. Andrzejewski
with Sheila Andrzejewski

Indiana University Press
Bloomington and Indianapolis

The paper used in this publication meets the minimum requirements of American National Standard for Information Sciences--Permanence of Paper for Printed Library Materials, ANSI Z39.48-1984.

Manufactured in the United States of America

Library of Congress Cataloging-in-Publication Data

An Anthology of Somali poetry / translated by B. W. Andrzejewski with Sheila Andrzejewski.
      p.   cm.
    Includes bibliographical references.
    ISBN 0-253-30462-8. -- ISBN 0-253-30463-6 (pbk.)
    1. Somali poetry -- Translations into English.   I. Andrzejewski, B. W. II. Andrzejewski, Sheila.
PJ2534.Z95E5   1993
893' .5--dc20   93-18386

1 2 3 4 5 97 96 95 94 93

To John William Johnson

with love and gratitude

CONTENTS

INTRODUCTION

When Sir Richard Burton visited Somalia in 1854 he found that a most striking characteristic of its inhabitants was their love of poetry. In his *First Footsteps in East Africa* he wrote:

> *The country teems with poets.... the fine ear of this people causing them to take the greatest pleasure in harmonious sounds and poetical expressions, where a false quantity or a prosaic phrase excite their violent indignation.*

This first report by an outsider on the poetic art of the Somali people was echoed by later travellers and scholars, so that the phrase 'a nation of poets' became current among people acquainted with the Horn of Africa.

Though much has changed in Somalia since the time of Burton, the popularity of poetry among all sections of society has not declined, and its paramountcy in the national culture is still unchallenged. Till the middle years of the twentieth century it remained an entirely oral art, for only in 1972 was an official system of writing established, but even today the spoken word remains supreme, for cassettes of old and new poems are constantly being taped, copied and recopied by Somalis whether living in their own country or abroad.

Anthologists are always open to the criticism that they have not chosen well. Somali readers will regret some of the omissions, though I think they will agree with the opinion of their compatriots whom I have consulted - connoisseurs and poets themselves - that all the poems are worthy of inclusion. I myself regret that there is no women's poetry here; I found it difficult, as a man, to collect any myself, and there is as yet little documentation on it, but there are hopeful signs that women researchers are taking on the task. Although there have been many women poets, their poetry seldom reached the public forum; in the traditional Somali society it would have been recited within a limited circle of family and friends, for women, though certainly not totally subjugated, had much less freedom in social interaction than men. The opportunities that men had to hone their debating and poetic skills in clan assemblies,   and to travel widely so that they could hear and compare poems from all parts of the country, were denied to women.   Above all, the cares of child-rearing, and the everlasting household chores, which included the construction and setting-up of the portable huts and the management of the herds of sheep and goats, meant that they had very little time for leisure pursuits.

When I was making my selection of poems I passed over many which, though much admired by Somalis, are so intimately entwined with local politics and clan feuds, past and present, as to be incomprehensible without a mass of explanatory material which would interfere with any enjoyment of the poetry. I chose poems which I think will have universal human appeal, and I believe that this anthology can be read, or browsed in, for its literary value alone.   The appendices are designed for those who want to learn more about Somali poetry and its context, and there is a bibliography of works on Somali culture in general.

The translations are as faithful as possible to the imagery of the originals and to their poetic message, but no attempt at all has been made to imitate the very complex versification.   This consists of a system of quantitative scansion, reminiscent of that in Classical Greek, and of a type of alliteration where the alliterative sound is sustained throughout the poem. Somalis identify a poem by its alliterative sound, its author and its theme and also on rare occasions by a particularly memorable line; here I have given the poems titles of my own invention,   to help the reader with identification and elucidation.

The anthology is presented in roughly chronological order, although the early poets can be placed only very approximately on a time scale. Such information as I have been able to gather is from oral sources, which I believe to be generally reliable, since Somalis attach great importance to the memorization of their genealogies and family histories. There is contemporary written information only in the case of Sayid Maxamed Cadbille Xasan, who was much discussed in European documents as the leader of the Dervish insurrection against the colonial powers on Somali soil between 1900 and 1920. He was then popularly known to his enemies as the "Mad Mullah", a sobriquet which is still remembered even by those who know little or nothing about him.

In 1854, as we have seen, Burton testified to the Somali devotion to poetry. It seems unlikely that the flowering of the poetic art that we find in the I9th and 20th centuries could have come suddenly into existence without being preceded by a long period of poetic activity, and yet almost nothing has survived from any earlier time. There is one poem - a meditation on the qualities of God - by a famous cleric, Sheekh Cali Cabduraxmaan, who probably lived in the I8th century, and some others which may be earlier, but these are anonymous and therefore very difficult to date. It is a mystery why the oral memory of Somalis does not extend beyond two centuries as far as poetry is concerned; perhaps further research will provide the answer, or perhaps we shall never know.

I have relied greatly on the help and guidance of Somali literary enthusiasts for the clarification of difficult or obscure passages in the poems, some of which are open to several interpretations, often widely divergent, with no certainty as to the best choice between them. In particular I am indebted to Maxamuud Sheekh Dalmar, a broadcaster and producer of literary programmes whose help has been particularly valuable in the final stages of this book, and to Cumar Aw Nuux, a former member of the Somali Academy of Arts and Sciences. Finally I remember with profound gratitude three eminent scholars who are no longer alive: Yuusuf Meygaag Samatar, Yaasiin Cismaan Keenadiid, and above all my dear friend and teacher, Muuse Xaaji Ismaaciil Galaal.

This volume is offered in the hope that the reader will be able to share something of the same enjoyment and enrichment that I have found since the day in 1950 when I first encountered Somali poetry.

B.W.A.

THE POEMS

RAAGE UGAAS

A l9th century pastoralist. He was the son of a powerful chief, and received an Islamic education at an itinerant college. He is considered by many Somalis to be the best of their poets, and his great popularity is mentioned in *Somalia e Benadir*, a book published in 1899 by an Italian explorer, Luigi Robecchi-Bricchetti. According to this account, Raage was known as a brave warrior and fell in battle in the l880s; if this is true, his "Old Age" is a poem of imagination, not experience.

To the Camels

The milch-camel

Morning has come, and she stirs and bustles.
She feeds her calf and then for a while
The flow of her milk is checked.

O you who make such a sound of beauty with your bellow
O you who so blithely give voice to your bubbling growl
It is you I call!

Now that the early hours of morn have passed
The cattle are loosed to seek their pastures
And the short-thighed sheep and goats find nearer grazing.

In the red light of morning there is glory in your eyes,
O you who ennoble with your presence
The family encampments and their pens full of livestock -
It is you I call!

When the sky is shorn of clouds
And the moon has doffed her halo,
Then parching heat dries up the land.
Many trees have lost their leafy shade
And even the *garas* leaves are green no longer.
The supply of milk grows scanty -
But on her one can still depend
For she will never fail her master.

It is you I call -
You who stretch your neck to find the leaves
That sprout on branches high above the ground,
When elsewhere there is nothing to be found   -
See! The round bowl is full of frothy milk!

The burden camel

Now people must prepare to move,
Quitting this waterless place to seek new pastures,
For the stars have moved into Daallali,
The season when no rain falls.

In dawn's red light the gelding is pursued and seized
And I tie his legs and make him kneel.
A softly-woven saddle-mat goes on his back
And over it another, all-encompassing,
Then the pole that stands so arrow-straight
In the centre of the hut -
All these I fasten tight with ropes.
Next up go kid and crimp-haired camel foal
And child too young to keep our pace,
And then on top I load more things -
Vessels in wicker carriers and big water flasks,
The kit for sewing skins together,
The tools to sharpen spearheads,
The daggers and the knives -
Side by side I place them on his back.
Lastly I add the roof-skins and the curved hut-poles
And once again I rope his burden fast.

I untie his legs
And up he rises, like a bustard startled into flight!

When the boy takes you by the leading-rope
You seem to plod along, slow-moving,
Yet who can keep up with you?
O soft-footed, soundless stalker -
It is you I call!

A Broken Betrothal

Night had fallen, the doors were shut and all men were asleep
Thunder resounded and the rain was echoing like a thousand rifle-shots
But still my shouts of lamentation could be heard -
People took them for the roar of an approaching lion.

Sore are my ribs, sore are the very bones of my spine -
Bones which are to men as a support-pole is to a hut -
And dammed up and unseeing are my eyes.
Only God knows fully the hurt that makes me wail like this!

A hawk cannot fly with an injured wing -
A broken-backed horse will not try to rise and run -
Many and loud are the growls of camels
When they are stricken by thirst.
A man whose eyes and rib-cage are not sound
Cannot avenge the wrongs that he has suffered,
And a man whose heart is afflicted with disease
Will not be making merry at a wedding-feast.

I grieve over my sorrow like a young girl
Whose mother has gone to rest in the other world
And whose father has brought home another wife
And made the girl sleep at the entrance of the new wife's hut.

I am a man whose betrothed was made to accept another -
I am a man who has seen a spring full of water
But whose thirst must stay unquenched forever.

A Horse Beyond Compare

When there's an equestrian poem to be made,
There are some men who are held back
As if confronted by a precipice.
Others, like me, are skilled in its art
And in the powers of good counsel it contains,

So I shall compose some praises for my horse Walhad
And start them with the sound of "waw".

Among horses and those who are their kin
One beast and another are not alike in worth.
Is Walhad not as swift as if he were hurled from a sling
From the top of a steep escarpment?
Does he not move with the speed of a message
Whose words are sent by wire?
Does he not respond to the reins
Like the well-set helm of a ship
Which is held in skilful hands?

His temper is hot, for that is his nature.
When he is taken to water I must lead him myself,
For if the man who holds the drinking-pail
Should motion him away ere he has had his fill
In a fury he will set upon that man
And upon any of the young lads standing near.
Is he not like a bull rhinoceros?

Fleet of foot, he wheels half-round and back again,
Like a roaming lion which snatches a beast from the herd
And as people shout, jumps to one side
And scares them off with his sudden leaps -
Is Walhad not like that?

His colour has the beauty of the sky
When it is spread out to dry after rain
With all its stains washed clean away.
He has the hue of an ostrich chick
Before its plumage whitens.
Is that hue not like the dawn
When the sun touches with its rays the thin high clouds?

If men are fighting somewhere, hand to hand,
And spears are hurled from one side to the other,
Through him I can restore the wholeness of my heart.

Is he not like a son given you by God
Or like a brother, blood of your parents' blood?

He brings me nourishment and good fortune
For when I ride him, whatever I am pursuing
Becomes like the roads running towards a well,
Roads fiercely pierced by spears of rain,
Or like a dry valley that has become a river in spate.

When I approach to free him from the hobbling-rope
He raises his head in a frenzy,
Then turning up his eyes he loses himself in wild leaping.
Is he not like a stargazing soothsayer
Or a divining sorcerer?

He deflects from my side
The spear that quarters the flesh,
The arrow tipped with black poison,
The hurled javelin swishing through the air
And the sling-shots of bullets.
Is he not like a renowned cleric,
Well-versed in reciting the Forty Suras,
Who for your protection will read
Those of the Forenoon and the Night
After you have slaughtered a ram for him?

When everyone is sleeping
And I take him from his pen
To leave him hobbled on the lea,
He does not stray far.
Is he not like a good young wife,
Who has spread for you a sleeping-mat
And now hovers round, attentive,
Accepting your advice and guiding words?

Riposte to a Young Opponent in a Poetic Duel

A lamb cannot ransom his mother from slaughter
Nor stop her being offered as meat for guests.
The new moon, only three days old,
May draw you from your settlement,
But its short-lived light is not enough
To guide your steps to town or village.

You may go to market and offer for sale
The feathers of a scavenger crow,
But however much you shout their praises -
Whatever blessings you intone -
Not one paltry *beeso* coin will you get for them,
Hard though you may bargain.

A mule may be a long-legged beast
But when he's on the practice-ground
He cannot match a horse.

The jenny-ass shuffles along with her burden,
Raising the dust as back and forth she journeys.
Trotting along behind her goes her colt,
But no load of milk or water does he carry -
All he does, that one, is break wind without pause.

The herd of cattle that tread their way
Along a dusty path ground down by hooves
Can sense if a lion has crossed their path,
Brushing out his footprints with his furry tail,
And even their bull, who claims to be so mighty,
Cannot give them courage then.

A boy, just circumcised, who thinks he is now of age
And sallies forth to challenge full-grown men to battle,
Is being driven onward by his sprouting hair.
But will that help him? Not one bit -
It is death he is playing with every time.

Old Age

Once I wore a fine russet cloak
And carried a shield of rhinoceros hide.
I was looked upon with admiration
As one of the best of humankind -
Is this not so?

Then my spine grew short and my back grew bent,
And did it not come to pass
That I had to stop and rest for the night
On a journey so short that shouting voices
Could have spanned the distance?
On the roads that are trodden by families on the move
I am passed by everyone along the way.
My weapons are all surrendered now
And my hand grasps nothing but a stick -
Is this not so?

The men begotten by men whom I myself begot
Withhold the support that is my due -
The women whom I married now wish me dead.

"Give me food!" I shout - do I not? - weeping like a child.
The shameful things against which I used to guard myself
Have now descended on me, as clear as the light of day -
Is this not so?

XIRSI GARAAD FAARAX 'WIILWAAL'

1801-1864 (according to the collector and editor of his poems, see Appendix V). He was a *garaad*, or chief, who inherited his office early in life and became well known for his hot temper and authoritarian tendencies, at the same time being much admired for his courage and cunning as a war leader, especially in a conflict with an Oromo clan led by their chief, Gaal Guray. His wit and wisdom and his penchant for spectacular practical jokes gave rise to many tales about him.

A Young Sultan Speaks to His People

If I present plainly, in a word or two,
A short account of myself and of my life
You will all of you have to say to me
With no one contradicting,
"You are telling the truth indeed!"

When I was a boy, with no share yet in the affairs of men,
I used to fill my ear, as if it were a vessel,
With the preaching of sheikhs,
With the advice of my old parents,
And with their words of guidance
Concerning the path of the Holy Faith.
Thus rightly counselled, I had an aim in mind.
A good cleric was what I would become!
I acquired for myself the implements of true piety -
A vessel for ablutions, the Holy Book,
And a very good mat for prayers -
Yet still you called me Wiilwaal, Crazy Lad!

And then it happened
That the fighting you were engaged in
Planted a desire in me
To show my solidarity with other men,
And if I had not bridled my horse Weyrax, the Rager
Nor held the shining spears and the shield of rhinoceros hide,
If I had not cried, "Onward, men!" as I launched an attack
At the first breaking of dawn's light,
And if I had not then hewn Guray into quarters -
The enemy would have overrun our country!

14

CALI BUCUL

A 19th century pastoralist.

Guulside, The Victory Bearer

There are three that share alike the name of horse,
And first there's the charger, that does not flinch
When javelins and arrows fly -
He's the one that enemies will cower from in fear.
Then there's the plodding nag, that's good for journeys made by night -
A useful mount for those advanced in years.
And lastly there's the mare, with which the other horses mate.
They know, these three, that all are of the same descent,
However much they differ in character and mien.
All have their respective grades of quality
And this is recognised at the assembly tree -
Is that not so, my noble people?

Now if I set out to give due praise
To my horse Guulside, the Victory Bearer,
And try to describe what he is like,
I must fall short in my account
For he is like a pool which fills with water
And fills itself again and yet again
And we will never fathom all his secrets.
Is that a fault on my part, O men, whoever you may be?

One evening is all the time he needs
To traverse the slopes of the Almis hills,
The plain of Harawo and the Gureys encampments.
Is he not as swift as a rain-bearing cloud at night?

At times of raging drought
When men lose hope for their herds,
You can ride out on Guulside
And he drives home looted camels.
Is he not like a man of mettle, raiding others' encampments?

15

At night, wherever he is put to graze,
His clamorous neighing wards off beasts of prey.
A mighty bellow he sends forth   -
Is he not like a lion, the leader of a pride of lions?

Wherever he is tethered
His fierce roaring protects that place
Against an enemy bent on mischief,
Against a powerful force,
Against a horde of warriors,
Against a troop of horsemen ready to attack,
Against marauders lurking round in bands.
No hunger comes into his homestead
People can sleep there soundly - can they not? -
For is he not like the death that massacres all creatures
And from which men flinch in horror?

Even when a dark and moonless night
Is enveloped by a falling sheet of rain
Whose drumming, and the roar of the wind,
Sets all living things a-tremble
And scatters their wits with fright,
He can detect the scent of a lurking thief.
Is he not then a soothsayer, a knower of hidden things,
A master of divination from the telling of the beads?

His body has not yet begun to grow old
But there is white at his nape and on his mane
See - is he not like an acacia tree in bloom?

AADAN-GUREY MAXAMED CABDILLE

A pastoralist who died at an advanced age c.1920.

Seventy and Ten Years

Seventy and ten are the years I have counted -
Is that not the truth?
Not one black hair can be seen on my head,
No more than on some youth who has powdered his locks
With ash which he mixed with chalk from a well.

Walking now fills me with such fear
That I judge it wiser to reach for what I want
Than trust to my feet to take me there.
I lean all my weight upon a stick
Like an old woman seeking alms from others of her ilk.

Once I wore with dignity a black-hemmed robe
But now I have to take a meagre length of cloth -
Two handspans wide, no more than that -
And fasten it with a girdle to another piece as scanty.

In the season of Dayr, with all its heavy heat,
I find no shade under the roof of a stout-poled hut.
The rising dust envelops me,
Just as it rises to cover an ostrich flock
That the cock-bird drives along before him.

I can find no repose for my neck, no ease
On wooden head-rest or pillow stuffed with hay
And instead, like a vagabond thief,
I must lay my ear against my arm.

My muscles are wasted, my skin is wrinkled
And assailed by illness as I am
My fingers no longer touch
The skirt-hems of my womenfolk.

There was a time, the time of my sojourn in Gidheys and Toglo,
When a great milk-vessel was mine, well-fashioned for my use.
There was a time when I could mount my powerful horse
And with my wealth give aid to martial ventures.
On night-time marches I stood out from all the others
As the man who could show them where the camels were.
We would launch a raid, stampeding the beasts,
And drive them back away from Toon -
The females, their fine nipples jutting,
Would run swiftly along in front of us.
Later, when all had been brought to a watered valley
We would slaughter a few of the gelded males
And then, when we came to divide between us
The beasts that we had captured,
If the men fell to squabbling over their shares
How well I knew ways of bringing them to order!

But that strength and that skill are lost to me now -
All lost.

FAARAX AFCAD

A pastoralist who died early in the twentieth century at an advanced age. He was well known for his sharp and critical wit.

Camel-Rustling - 1

This poem and the next arose from an old custom among poets of imitating, in jest, the boasts of vainglorious warriors.

I summoned a band of kinsmen
For a raid that was to be launched,
And we chose only champion warriors
And the best of our young blood.
We rode throughout the long and wind-swept night
And then, since the men were hunched with cold,
I set ablaze a log of wood to give them warmth.

The scouts were now assigned their horses,
A white-tailed piebald and a bay,
And soon they sighted one another,
The men we sent and those who in their turn
Were on the watch for our approach.
They loomed up from afar, seeming to us
Like a mountain, or a blazing fire.

The noise of battle resounded like a downpour of rain in spring,
And bent on camel-booty our young men burst into their camp.
In no time we had put to fright the females of the herd
And driven them towards our side -
They bolted when we struck their shoulders with our whips.
Horses reared and jumped, horses of good descent from sire and dam,
And a stallion known for his fierce neighing galloped forward,
Dalaq, dalaq, dalaq!

On the milch-camels the fibre bands were loose and dangling
That once bound tight the hindmost nipples of their udders.
Their owners were aflame with anger,

19

They who had known the joy of milk
From beasts just lately calved,
And when they saw us in the open ground
They poured on us a volley of their javelins.
We asked each other, "Shall we let the camels go?"
But we are seasoned fighters, so instead
We drove them to one side
And then we stood our ground.
Straightway short spears were hurled at us,
Shafts swishing as they flew,
But I had taken as booty a shield
That was whiter than any cloud
And I killed their foremost champion.

When a band of them tried to retrieve their herd
I turned again, and soon we routed them
And sent them off stumbling over the stumps of trees.
I captured a horse, a bay roan that trotted behind my mount,
While with our whips we urged along a goodly mare I had taken -
Nor did we allow the camels to stray by running to and fro.

O what numbers of men I have killed
For the sake of those beasts of the excellent udders!

QAWDHAN DUCAALE

A pastoralist who was active as a poet in the first half of the twentieth century.

Camel-Rustling - 2

I gathered the men as dawn's first light was glimpsed
And we harnessed the horses ready for the raid.
Skin bottles were checked and filled with camel's milk.

On such a venture one does not make a stop
To rest in the shade from midday heat,
So on we rode, talking and exchanging banter.
On our night halt we took care to mute our voices,
And when the men complained of the cold
I warmed them with my words.
We resolved to saddle up in good time on the morrow,
Keeping before us the aim for which we had set out,
So at dawn we caught our horses without trouble.

Mounted once more, we started at an easy trot,
The pace which had always ensured success for me,
And command was entrusted to one young in years
Who was yet gifted with mettle and propitious omens.
Out of our valiant band two scouts were sent ahead
And with the sun already past its highest point
Our horsemen stretched their necks and saw the camels.

Now began the uproar of battle,
Resounding like bursts of heavy rain.
In an attack one does not hold back
And we drove the camels towards our side -
They stampeded as our sticks struck their shoulders.
Some of our horses shied away, not yet obedient to the rein,
But the men whose war-steeds were well-trained
Outflanked and rounded up the herd.

Then the warriors confronting us gave ground
And sheered off to one side.
I gave my horse to the men to hold, and seized my shield.
Two long spears, the shield and my tattered garment
Were all my equipment as I bounded forward.
Blood, red as berries, drenched the cloth
That later I gave to those who had lagged behind,
And the birds of prey, whose fare it was,
Tore at the flesh of our enemies for their food.

Words of alarm were carried to the camels' owners
And they mounted their carefully nurtured steeds.
When they descried us in the open plain
A volley of javelins was poured upon us
But we are men who have always been used to vigilance
And our short spears were there at the ready.
For Walhad these had been nights without pasture
While I prepared him for the battle,
But when I struck him with my whip
He joined the charge in the way I had taught him
And soon a horse I had captured was trotting behind us.

Concerning a man of small achievements
There is room for contradiction,
But as for me, I wrought disaster on those men -
Truly valour is a gift from God!
We drove them back, far back,
That band that came to retrieve what we had looted.

Going home, on a road swept clean by the winds,
I chanted an equestrian poem in triumph.
Like men on a migrating trek
We followed the camels at an easy pace
As they swung their legs, with the cloths all dangling
That had slipped from the foremost nipples of their udders.

Many young men have arisen now,
They are as numerous as bushes in the scrub,
But it is to me that they defer

When it comes to the rallying words of war.
Just as did Heeban once - that lion of a man -
So now do I excel all others.
Xuseen, too, will never be baulked on the field of battle -
As a bird of prey takes his quarry
So did he make an end of Leefleef
And bring the tale of that man's glory to a halt.
You and I, Xuseen, we two, are famous now at limeey,
The watering-place that lies by the river.
O you who are the very image of a bird of prey,
May Death long let you alone!

CALI JAAMAC HAABIIL

A pastoralist who died in the middle years of the 20th century. He was a prominent spokesman of his clan and a strong opponent of Maxamed Cabdille Xasan, whose poems are included in this anthology.

The Death of a Friend

O Faarax, as I tossed from side to side, deserted by sleep,
Black-headed vipers thronged into the bed where I was lying
And my teeth forsook the food that had been laid before me.
May they be bereft of kin, those messengers of Xirsi's death!
May their fate be to end their lives with all their children dead,
Those women who brought me news of disaster and despair!
The sun has now set on the family that dwelt in the plain of Booc.
Men have always died, I know,
But grievous has been the blow this death has dealt me.

Six thoughts I have concerning him -
Am I brooding too much over them? I do not know.
The first is that when bands of men fought hand to hand,
With each side seizing camels from the other
Then sending men to rescue them again,
Or when a raiding party we had mustered
Rode long and hard and came at last to battle
While quaking cowards scurried to and fro -
How skilful were his tactics,
How he dodged and weaved and closed around the foe!
Am I brooding too much over this? I do not know.

In a perplexing case about a convoluted matter
When the arbitrators were all of them at variance,
And the elders, gathered under the council tree,
All differed in their opinions, their heads unyielding, stiff,
And even after much debating no consensus could be reached
It was he, a softly-spoken man, who would make a speech of wonder
And all would fall in with his judgment.
Am I brooding too much over this? I do not know.

If he was with us when, of a sudden, guests arrived -
May he be blessed in his grave with the joys of Paradise! -
He would seek to lessen our burden as hosts
And would, that very afternoon,
Take some of the visitors into his own household,
Where he himself would bring the bedding mats for them,
Carrying the load on his shoulder, as is men's way.
The food spread out for them was plentiful,
As plentiful, it seemed, as water of torrent or pool.
His talk was ever free and friendly -
Not for him the miser's grimace, that bares one molar in a laugh.
Am I brooding too much over this? I do not know.

The spring rains are falling, wedding-drums have sounded
And meetings of importance have been called
By noble men and lineages of consequence.
It is a time when pacts of mutual aid are made
By men who sit around in circles.
But since I have been left without his support
I declare such places are empty now for me -
Empty too the encampment from which he would come riding.
Am I brooding too much over this? I do not know.

A pitch-dark night cannot be compared in usefulness
To one that is lit by a bright full moon,
Even though one night is sibling to the other.
Just so are there some men who are hard as oryx horn
In their unjust treatment of their kin.
But he was as meek with them as is the camel
That fetches water and does not shun
The skin on which the load is put.
He would offer them, too, the shaded seat
That lies atop the camel-pack.
Am I brooding too much over this? I do not know.

By God, this man with his shoulders like an arch
Was truly a fence to guard the family encampments.
His fame had spread to unbelievers and Muslims alike
And he was renowned from West to East.

Tall and fine of stature, he was an iron shield to protect us.
Am I brooding too much over this? I do not know.

I know that men have to leave this world, -
Which anyway is in its final stage -
Men have been leaving it, indeed
From the day of Muhammad's death until this hour,
And yet I have been burning with resentment
Over the loss of this magnificent man.

I accept your will, O God, that is forever just.
There are no folk living who will not die
And I have greatly erred through my rebellious grief.
Do not cut me off, O God, but set me at the side of the Prophet
On that Day when all people will be gathered in.

MAXAMED CABDILLE XASAN

c.1860-1921. He received a very thorough Islamic education in Somalia and later travelled to Arab countries, where he further advanced his knowledge and became familiar with the revivalist trends in Islam at the time. On his return he organized a Dervish Movement to oppose the foreign powers (British, Italian and Ethiopian) who ruled the Somali territories, and proved to be an astute war leader, fighting for about twenty years until his defeat in 1920 and death in exile a year later. He was an outstanding poet, using his poems as an effective form of propaganda, and he is often called simply the Sayid, ("Lord" or "Master") the title his followers gave him. There are several works on his life, the most important being by Abdi Sheikh-Abdi and Said S. Samatar (see Appendix IV).

A Fine War Horse

When men are summoned from afar to fight,
To march there would be weary work indeed,
But Walhad spreads his back for me
As if he were a soft skin bedding-mat.
Does he not act as a good wife does?

The skin flask holding camel's milk -
Weeto's milk, which fills one to the full -
The fashioned saddle, the bit, the ornamented straps,
The glinting bridle, the tasselled halter
Which he tosses up and down,
The thonged whip, the shield of wrought rhinoceros hide,
The long spear chosen from my stock of spears
And myself, who am speaking to you now -
All these he carries on his back.

He moves with a swinging gait,
The gait of a bull elephant when angered.
Do not expect sedateness from him -
Is he not an afreet, an out and out demon?

If I mount him at first light of dawn
And under the hot sun ride on throughout the day
He is a cooling wind in himself.
Is he not the light breeze of evening?

27

But if we set out on a long night's journey
He protects me from the cold damp air.
Is he not a mantle that is spread around me?

When the camels have gone forth to graze
And an attack is made when they stop to feed,
Is he not like a javelin being hurled
As he bounds out from among a hundred companions?

He will stretch out his forelegs to seize what he wants
He grasps it with his hooves.
Is he not a lion clutching with its claws?

Where there is fighting and the taking of booty
And when men take aim and fire off their bullets,
He can dodge them - is he not an agent of God?

When I ride into battle he manoeuvres adroitly
And stays unscathed by hurtful blows.
Is he not an ostrich chick escaping danger?

He brings destruction to great men
He cuts off the life of the brave
He recovers stock that was captured.
Is he not hot death itself?

He carries off camels for himself
He takes Weeto in milk and Weris in calf.
Is he not a powerful lord?

When people are growing weak with hunger
In a place where no grazing can be found,
He feeds them to satiety.
Is he not the rain that autumn brings?

Through him I profit from the Holy Word
And from the Four who bear the Message.
Is he not a saint of blessings?
He is better than all the goods this world provides.

I have made him my father, who gave me life -
A brother, too, he is to me.
Is he not the means of reaching Paradise?

There are times when I do not see him, and then I die,
Overwhelmed by the troubles and worries of this world.
Is he not my very heart?

In time of drought I kill rams for him
And for him I cut the choicest meat.
Is he not a cleric who comes to me as a guest?

I take ghee to anoint his coat
On flanks and withers and head.
Is he not a male child begotten by me?

I can never be without him -
He stays in the very courtyard of my hut
Or in the zariba, close at hand.
Is he not my beloved first-born son?

With his brawny neck and back
He is like a beautiful city.
No speck of dirt would ever be found on him -
Is he not like shining silk?

When he turns on all four legs
He moves his fetlocks carefully
And with circumspection rocks his body round.
Is he not a sheikh in a state of ritual purity?

He swaggers as he swings along,
Shaking his body with a bobbing trot.
Is he not a commoner become proud?

His mouth is a pool of water cleft in two
And the bit that makes it whole again
Must be put in deftly.

Is he not an awesome invocation
Of the omnipotence of God?

His gaze is ever vigilant,
And those sparks which glint in his eyes -
Are they not like lightning flashes?

Even through a distant haze
He can see the fluttering of birds
And descry the smallest thing that stirs.
Is he not a sharp-eyed mongoose?

If he hears the buzz of shouting from afar
He at once pricks up his ears, alert.
Is he not a watchful listener for news?

He can catch any sound in an instant
Though it may come from a place too far away
For even the loudest cry to carry.
Is he not the deadly telegraph wire?

See how he flourishes his testicles,
How he swishes his tail and the tuft of his mane!
Is he not fashioned like an eland?

His neck is as strong as a knee-joint -
Is his back not as wide as an encampment courtyard,
As a clearing swept quite clean?

His stall is set apart under a thatch of leafy boughs
And when I shut him in he is mad with rage
Yet he does not show it - he holds himself quite still.
Is he not an astonishing creature?

If I thrust my knees into his sides
He tosses his reins in a frenzy
As a wild fury seizes him.
Is he not an aroused rhinoceros?

At sunset he is sent to search for straying calves
And then he walks with caution, as if lame.
Is he not a portly elder?

When he canters towards me, his hoofbeats
Resound like thunder rumbling in a valley.
Is he not the sky when storm-clouds gather?

When with a strong rope I tether him,
He moves around with care.
Is he not someone anxious to avoid being hurt?

As we ride forward along the road
He does not thwart my plans.
Is he not a wise man?

He tarries in one place, in another he crosses the rivers -
He is gone for a while, then here he is again!
Is he not a jinn?

Widely he roams in far-off places,
In those foreign lands which God has made so vast.
Is he not a swift-blowing wind?

However hard his exertions, he never loses flesh
Nor does his body weaken.
Is he not an opulent and ample-bodied man?

However long he keeps up an attack
Never will he drink water that mud has blackened
Nor milk that bitterness has spoiled.
Is he not an pious and unspotted man?

He drinks from deep wells
And shelters under leafy awnings.
He comes to the assembly -
Is he not a turbanned governor?

I have fashioned my words well and now I stop.
Are his praises not my duty,
My obligatory prayer tasks,
My voluntary devotions?

A Land of Drought

All these were mine -
Camels newly-calved, cattle plump of flesh,
A stock of sheep and goats,
Skimmed milk enough to plunge my mouth in deep and gulp it down,
An abundance of wealth,
And ghee churned in a great jar made of camelskin.
I had the meat of a gelded camel to eat,
Red meat and white and pieces of fat,
And the recesses of my hut were filled with silk and fine cloth.
Those were prosperous days when I stayed in the hills of Ayl!

It was not my idea that I should move away from there
And troubles broke upon me
As soon as my camels were loaded for the journey.
Men who did not know the will of the Lord
Poured away the contentment I had enjoyed -
It was they who forced me to come to the Nugaal
For I myself received no inner guidance in the matter.
I was not pleased with the plan, but they drove me onwards -
Why else would I have moved my household
From its dwelling-place there on the hill?

As I set down my family on this plain of Doodi
I saw that even a goat would go hungry here.
The herds were undone to find themselves amidst this bitter scrub
And the strongest of camels have weakened for lack of sustenance.

I uprooted myself from a place where rich grass grew for me.
In those days there was lush growth wherever I turned my face -
In those days a *jeerin* fruit, big as a man's head,
Would be put to cook in heated sand for me -

In those days I needed to assign for grazing
A mere quarter of the grass that was newly springing.
Had I but stayed in the Hawd
I would not now be afflicted by grinding want.
And yet how warmly they recommended this forsaken region,
Where the ranging beasts of prey pace swiftly round me
And where if a rotting carcass meets my sight
It proves to be that of a man or a woman or a child.

This is a place without one patch of ground
Where the wild game herds could graze,
It is a place where beasts must pluck
Small mouthfuls here and there of scrub and straw,
It is a place of no abiding use,
A place where teeth will find no food to chew!

Treason

During the Sayid's Dervish war a band of conspirators at headquarters plotted to overthrow him, but the plot was discovered. Some conspirators were executed, others fled, and the Sayid, shattered by their disloyalty, expressed his feelings in this poem, addressed to an army commander who had remained faithful, Suudi Shabeele.

O Suudi, your wealth has accrued in Heaven, now listen to my words!
I rest my confidence in you - may God grant you peace
And may not a word of what I say miss its target in you.
Sugar, wheat mixed with honey and dressed with ghee,
Dishes with aromatic sauces and the dates which give them colour,
Fresh camel's milk, a fatted he-goat slaughtered,
Its ribs well-spiced -
Such was the fare I offered to those men for sustenance.
In the deep of the night I took them provisions for their journey.
Liberally were they treated, in very truth,
And this is what they did to me!

I raised them to parity with sultans and honoured them.
They were placed in charge of the camel threesomes -
Sucklings, dams and foster-dams -

And the allotment of grain was in their hands.
With ease I granted them whatever they desired.

I entertained them, offering them beds to sleep on
I prepared for them an array of mats and fine cloth screens
I apportioned to them secluded parts of the enclosure
And I gave them girls in marriage, all nobly beautiful.

These were the men whom I cosseted
These were the men I protected from even a mote of dust.
I guarded them in the conflicts of war
And in their own concerns.
On young and old I bestowed my bounty -
I doled out countless grazing beasts
And camel threesomes by the hundred.

Choice foals and gelded war-horses
Were given them by my orders.
I handed over stacks of arms,
Martini rifles and bullets aplenty.
For them I offered up my prayers
For them I led the chorus of Koranic recitations
And I sought forgiveness for them from the Prophet.

I deemed them trustworthy and sincere, my close kin,
And I encamped in their enclosures
And in the clearings beside their homesteads,
But now, through the suffering they have brought on me
I have become forgetful and distracted in my prayers.

O men, how vehemently beats my heart!
I did not expect from these my kinsmen,
Nor from anyone who was close to me,
An hour like the one today.
All Somalis are bitter bane and poison to me now!
Ignoble men and thieves have pounced on me -
May their ancestors be damned -
To the shame of their clans those blackguards betrayed my trust
And even my own brothers-in-law mistreated me!

There was no rancour between me and Faarax,
Yet he stealthily moved away to distant pasture land.
It was surely Satan who caught hold of him,
Leading him down a ladder from the upper air
And despatching him to Berbera.
If he had had within him any sentiments of holy joy
He would never have prostrated himself before the unbelievers.
The clan of Samatar Khalaf - may they be held in fetters -
Failed to be guided by good counsels.
The young men whom I nurtured have turned into villains,
Plotting against me when I was being sincere with them.
All beings that breathe have become hostile to me.
If they rush at me with abusive harangues, then so be it,
But I did not expect Qoriyow to ready his spear to assail me.

Even though I apportioned to Axmed Fiqi
The best meat from the breast,
Even though I showered him with favours,
I received no recompense for the bounty I bestowed.
Never can I sleep for the malice he exudes -
It must have been his evil star and Saturn's power
That caused him to appear in the plain of Ciid
And set upon me like a frenzied beast of prey
So that I was forced to ask myself,
"Did the Europeans send him against me?"

He deceived me with professions of ascetic piety,
That levied soldier of the foreign power,
And only two days since, the imbecile,
He gave his help to the unbelievers.
His disgraceful deeds now number thirty - nay, more!

God has ever made it my portion in life,
Whether in my youth or now that I am an elder,
To endure sorcerers, who are my foes.
But even the men I had bound to friendship
Brought me misfortune, every one of them!

But since in these days no soul can be sincere and loyal
It is pointless to wake up at night in terror
Like someone possessed by a demon.
Therefore, O God, I patiently put my trust in you -
Bestow now your favour on my counsels!

A Terrible Journey

The Sayid had been promised by a Boqor, or Sultan, of one of the regions of Somalia, that he and his troops would be given shelter there against their enemies. They undertook an arduous trek in the hot, dry season, only to find that the Boqor had reneged on his promise, and they had to retreat. The precise historical background of this event and the motives of the Boqor have not been firmly established. The opening words of the poem are addressed to Xuseen Maxamuud Faarax (q.v.), a faithful friend who was often entrusted with the memorizing of his poems.

One should not utter contentious words, Xuseen,
And in any case you at least are a dear friend to me
For you did not defect when fools decamped in fright,
You did not run to the Emperor when your kinsmen fled.
They belong in hell, those men who do not fight the infidels,
And I assure you, by the words of the whole Koran,
That that is where they will surely go.
But you loaded your camels and came to me
At the very time your kinsmen were moving off to Janan.
A man who is not of your mettle is nothing but a weakling!
I have turned away from others
But to you I am a bosom friend,
And I shall comfort and sustain you
In the hard days of the season of *jiilaal.*

A vision of the welcome spring rains, a symbol of his poem.

A trailing of rosy light, hazy wisps high above,
Towering precipices of clouds, flashes of lightning,
Thunder reverberating, flood-water rushing in spate,
The earth and air vibrating with the sounds ahead,
Last night's heavy rain that roared like a falling meteorite,
Showers pouring down, the splendour of spring rains,
A pond filled to the brim,

Pools overflowing, hollows swelling with water,
The parched land sprouting grass, thickets rustling -
Like this will your longings be allayed,
As when a camel slakes her craving
When the salty water is poured out for her,
For I shall entertain you
With a poem like a precious stone.

Listen to my words then -
Tonight I shall pour them out for you!

The poet's life of contentment and plenty before he began his journey.

When I was staying in my homestead,
I and the troops who were my kin,
No man ever uttered to me
One single hurtful or offensive word
No one came to me who would have robbed me
Of even the smallest scrap of leather.
I studied the commentaries of the Jalaals,
I pursued religion through ecstatic states.
In the quiet comfort of my own headquarters
I joined the congregation in their communal prayers.
Whatever I wished for was given to me in full -
I had all the good things of this world,
Frothy sour milk I drank, and curds,
And I was never deprived of food when I wanted it.

Then folly possessed me
And cheated me of the jewel of my life-force,
Me - a man not devoid of high purpose,
And ready to climb the mountain peaks,
Who like an unbroken he-camel
Has never known the touch of a bridle!
But when the words that called me to come
Were uttered, and prevailed on me,
It was by an ordinance of God
That I was compelled to do what I did.

The poet's journey takes him through a forest, where trees and bushes impede his progress and prowling beasts, spies, marauders and finally snakes add to the dangers.

There was a thicket of *xagar* trees,
There were *jaleefan* and *qurac*, and the cutting *jinow*,
The close-growing *galool*, and the *sarmaan*
With its pods that whistle in the wind,
The swinging and recoiling *jimbac*,
The intertwining *jiiq* trees,
The *jiic* shrub and the *siiq* wild fig,
The stinging *jillab* nettles,
The shrivelled *jowdheer* gum tree,
Jagged branches inflicting grievous pain,
The *jirme* with its thorns,
The *jiiqjiiq* with its prickles,
The *jeerin* and the *yooco* flame tree,
The *qaroon*, the *jaaful* and the *seerin*,
And tree-stumps everywhere along the path I trod.
Journeying through the night I tore my way
Through tick-infested bushland
And I stumbled and fell
As the ground dropped steeply beneath my feet.
A lion roared, its front paws as thick and rough
As an old pack-saddle.
He followed me along the track of footprints
That I myself was following -
I could hear his steps behind me,
And time after time I turned to look back.
Spies were lurking on either side,
Watching as I made each step in fear,
Stretching out my arms before me.
With strips of bark I warded off
A wild dog and a hairy-tufted rhino,
A leopard shrieked at me, possessed by jinns,
And suddenly a whole crowd of beasts of prey
Were playing and sporting there.
Stalking marauders appeared far off,
Prowling in the scrub of the waterless plain,
And then a hunter passed close by,
Cautiously crouching as he walked.

I came to a stretch of broken ground
Where not one family camp was   pitched,
I trudged across a waterless land
Where the very air engendered thirst.
The francolin screamed at sight of me
And the ill-omened bustard uttered his piteous cries.
I trekked along a drought-stricken road
The wind of the *xagaa* season licking my face.
My eyes lost their power as without cease I peered about me,
And I had to turn my face from the springing, whipping branches.

Marching from early morning, marching again in the afternoon,
I pressed on towards the East.
With every swing of arm or leg
I could hear the clamour of my cracking joints.
On that long journey I counted each weary span I trod
As thorns shed by the trees snapped under my feet.

How prickly and sore was my skin -
What distress I suffered -
What sharp blows to my ankles and pains in all my tendons!
Stumbling and tripping I hit one foot against the other -
Spine and sinews were racked by the hurt inflicted on them
And I even broke a toe on a tree-stump buried in the ground.
I tore through euphorbias that crackled like crickets,
Through caltrops that pricked and entangled.
I was exhausted by the trek, parched with the heat and hungry
And as I marched on and on my body grew lean and gaunt.

Springing, I snatched my foot from a *jilbis* and a *good*
Only to step on an *abees* as it lay, coiled and scaly-skinned,
While the snake that goes *chrak-chrak-chrak* dashed into me
As it clattered on its way.
I fell to the ground exhausted
Yet I could not rest where I lay,
And moaning, I bent my limbs, then stretched,
Then bent them once again.
Through hunger and thirst my gullet was blocked
And in no way could I free it.

When the morning star appeared I resumed my march,
Trudging to the ring of my sandals on the ground.
On that early morning journey
My countenance grew haggard
And there was a roaring in my ears
As loud as a falling meteorite.
But I got into this plight myself
And the body that I injured was my own.
The fate I am suffering was ordained for me by the Lord
And driven by want I had to drain it to the dregs.

Had there been no answer from the Boqor
I would not have craved for the coast as camels crave for salt.
My body would not have suffered hurt
If he had told me to stay away,
But it was my affection for him
That drew me to the sand-dunes by the sea.

That journey across the steep escarpments
Must have been decreed for me by God
For only an ignorant man does not know
Whither he is being taken by a leading-rope,
But it was the Boqor dangling before me a shawl of honour
That brought this trial upon me.

There was a time when he and his men
Had gifts from me of horses and bellowing camels,
Herds of humped cattle and flocks of sheep and goats,
And I untied prodigious sums of money
And crammed their pockets full.
For them I slaughtered gelded camels, big of flank,
And cut them the choicest, fattest meat.
For them great dishes of millet
Were in friendship filled and filled again,
And vessels brimmed with milk from camels, newly-calved,
That crooned and murmured to their young.
I gave them splendid brides
And huts divided by screens of skin,
I offered them jars of honey and well-smoked meat to eat

For them I burnt *jaawi* incense and filled pots full of tea.
These were men whom at the assembly-ground
I took care never to offend.

But never did I expect any reward from them for all I did,
For my meed will come from God alone.

.   .   .   .

No matter what plans a man may make,
The outcome will be decided not by him
But by the constraining forces of the times.

Folly

A clan hostile to the Sayid had attacked the Dervishes, who not only defeated them but took many camels as booty. The Sayid addresses the young leader of the beaten clan.

You know nothing, young man, you are a fool!
Your head is choked up with stupidity
Else you would not surely be so useless.
You will be lost - but I take refuge from these matters
With the Everlasting One.

You try to compete with men whose peer you will never be,
You think you can attack the clouds around the Heavenly Throne.
But your real standing and your lack of strength
Will thwart you in your purpose.

The potion of bitter myrrh I mixed for you
Is dripping from your nostrils.
The exhaustion you are suffering now
Has come from your defeat that day.
Your feet are weary, the skin is peeling from your heels.

If you and your warriors do not mean to fight,
The best thing is to sulk, as women do.

Desist then, for you are good for nothing -
May the winds of the air now spirit you away!

Perhaps the Trumpet Has Sounded

During the Dervish insurrection the whole of Somali society was torn apart by war. The Sayid laments over this disaster and over the moral degradation for which he blames his Somali opponents, accusing them of supporting the colonial powers.

Grievous times are now upon us, times of death and woe.
The sky has turned to smoke,
There is uproar and shrieking, columns of dust, attacks -
In truth this world is smouldering with strife
And with forebodings of war.
Friends part and head their different ways,
Close kinsmen align themselves in rival factions
And pierce each other's flesh with spears.
Loyalty to one's kin, and respect for the parents of one's spouse,
Are ways of life which are now dead.

Men run wildly about in pursuit of vengeance,
Supporting the unbelievers, who offer them grain for food.
Foreign soldiers are the ones they choose
In preference to the Prophet, on whom be peace.
They are besotted with these tufted officers
And declare themselves men who belong to Swayne,
Meekly accepting his rule in the places where he makes his camp.
The holy man, honoured receiver of visits and gifts,
Wakes up at night in terror
And learned clerics become forgetful in their prayers
As Saturn takes on a sinister likeness to Mars.
They no longer truly heed the dire requitals of the world to come
They cease to remember the day, that was like a propitious star,
When the Holy Law was placed on high.
When they enlist in the strangers' army -
May God smite them with torments -
They come to see unbelievers as a source of goodness
When instead they should invoke against them
The protection of the Lord.

People neglect the words which God revealed
And treat them lightly.
No heed is taken of the Month of Fasting
Nor of the prayers that are prescribed.
They give not even one small measure of wheat
In the alms that are obligatory to all,
And as they make ready for the Holy Pilgrimage
They prepare for their arrow-tips deadly bane and poison.

The man is now a pauper who in the past
Had herd upon herd of animals in his zariba.
Those who have grown old are not spared,
Nor even the defenceless child.
Evil plots are hatched, and night and day
Shameless robberies are committed.
Each dawn brings outrage and injustice
Wreaked by men upon each other.
They roam the streets, invoking God
With oaths of triple force,
But it is lies they are spreading - only lies!

The observance of the Tradition
And of binding obligations,
The feeding of guests,
The giving of charitable gifts on feast days,
Wise discourse and Sufi piety,
Forgiveness for the sake of the Faith -
These happy practices of holy joy are all forsaken
And goodness now is spurned.

Emissaries had approached the Sayid with rich gifts and offers of girls in marriage, trying to persuade him to give up his holy war, but the Sayid rejects these temptations.

A beautiful girl, a bridal hut with a store of robes,
A sleeping recess set apart behind a screen,
A vessel in a sturdy wicker frame,
Thirty gourds, containers full to the brim,
A bedding mat, an incense burner well alight, scented smoke,
Fine garments made of silk,

Cloth they call *bafto* and *khali* and *suuti*,
A heavy-bodied steed, a supple foal, a long-maned mare,
Camel threesomes of suckling, dam and foster-dam,
A stud-beast broad of rib, a corpulent gelding, graceful foals
And a heifer that was mated with a vigorous and excellent male,
Cattle galore, sheep and goats thronging -
The clearing round the encampment was full of them.
But what is all this if one does not depend on God for his bounty?
If a man who provides sustenance is treated in an unjust way,
If people refuse to greet you when you fall below them in fortune,
If a man steals the property with which he was entrusted,
If a man whom you took up and helped now treats you vilely,
If when you are honest no one values you for it,
If a man who leads an ascetic life in the pursuit of virtue
Is challenged to a fight without any cause,
If men who are holy and deserving of recompense
Are stripped of their woollen cloaks,
If men who are not stupid are still not respected,
If people who once depended on your aid
Now turn and plot against you,
If men to whom you owe nothing, not one small coin, one *saaq,*
Still force you to roam in the heat of the sun,
If loyalty between marriage-kin is observed no longer,
If good behaviour brings no profit,
If friends who once were true ignore your call for aid,
And if a man who has obeyed the precepts of virtue
Still has to wait patiently for God to give him justice -
Then, O men, perplexing times are upon us, seasons of woe!

One shudders at the happenings in the world as it is now.
Perhaps the Trumpet has sounded and the Last Hour is nigh!
I shall not have long to wait, then,
For the fate that my lost peers suffered,
Those friends, lofty as clouds, who were cut down.

Surely it must be that thirty years ago
There was on this very day some great disaster
And events are happening again that happened then!

No integrity can be found in any breathing creature
No goodness can be got from them except by shameful means.
How is it possible then that I could have secured my interests?
A man such as I is much more than a child -
Bear in mind that I am an elder,
You who expect me to behave like a youth!
I can recognise the true voice
Of those who speak with tongues so smooth.
If someone seeks to ensnare me
By pouring out amiable attentions
I must be tethered fast or I shall bolt,
Affrighted by the *saar* leaves dangling there before me.
I shall evade the pit-trap and the primed snare,
I shall turn away from everyone, the old and the young.
They may caress me but they will not deceive me -
Like a timid gazelle I shall take fright and flee
If a sound from them so much as reaches my ear.

Sugar, wheat and honey dressed with ghee,
Meat with its juices, cut in slices -
I shall reject all this that they are using to entrap me.
I shall listen, to be sure, to the man
Who offers me a girl in marriage,
Promising me a wedding feast in the household of a sultan,
And I shall say to him, "Arise and go home now,
And the day after tomorrow I shall come to you" -
But instead I shall sneak into the thick bushland of Sool
And make my way to pastures far away from here.

Footprints will show a wanderer's path
As much as does a rising cloud of dust
And to take a route through sandy ground
Would lead to sure detection,
But stony ground holds danger, too,
For my feet could stumble on the slippery rocks
And I must steer clear of all these perils.

If elders descend on the clearing by my encampment,
Or on the path beside my home,

Bringing provisions, animals and shares of wealth,
I shall take nothing from them - I shall turn away.
Even were my life to stretch to nine hundred years
It could never enter into my heart
To follow these men whom Satan sent,
These thieves who were none of my inviting.
Even if swords and rifles are taken up against me and bullets shot,
Even if my enemies fry me in the Saqara zone of Hell,
Even if I am hunted everywhere, from here to Suakin,
Even if I am taken to Berbera, or to Aden Barracks,
Even if I am put before the Europeans and shouted at,
I shall not listen to any words but the words of Scripture
That are written on a slate.

You who are Peace, O God,
Let me not transgress the holy precepts!
One day I shall be freed from my predicament
And be delivered from the dangers that beset me.
O God, I have waited in vain for help from others -
Do not now cast me aside, O God!

A Prayer for Maryam

Composed when Maryam, one of the Sayid's wives, was seriously ill.

O God, you to whom worship is given,
It is to you I turn, a poor suppliant,
It is before you that I lay my request.
Bring unto us, O God, relief in Maryam's plight.

She has been a mother to Muslims, wherever they might be.
To those fleeing from danger, countless thousands of them,
She offered a refuge, without thought for herself.
Bring unto us, O God, relief in Maryam's plight.

She has been the very meeting-place for guests,
For our kinsmen who were old, our women and our young ones,
For others like them, the defenceless ones,

Mothers and children, all these deserving folk -
Bring unto us, O God, relief in Maryam's plight.

XUSEEN MAXAMUUD FAARAX, known as 'XUSEEN DHIQLE'

He was the chief memorizer of the poems composed by the Sayid (Maxamed Cabdille Xasan, q.v.) and a devoted follower of his during the Dervish rising. He probably died towards the middle of the twentieth century.

The Lion's Share

After the defeat of the Dervish rising in 1920, and the death a year later of the Sayid its leader, some of his adherents sought asylum with the Arsi, a Muslim Oromo clan who lived in Ethiopian territory; among these refugees was Naado, a widow of the Sayid, Sheekh Yuusuf his brother, Jamaad his sister and the poet, Xuseen Maxamuud Faarax. The refugees had to surrender their weapons and possessions to their hosts, on whom they were entirely dependent for sustenance and safety. A member of the chiefly family of the Arsi, called Cali Diniqo, married Naado, while the paramount chief, Nuux Maxamuud Dhaadi, asked for the hand of Jamaad. She wished to refuse him but her brother, who was her legal guardian, reluctantly consented to the marriage, since he knew Nuux's autocratic temperament and feared the consequences of rejection. He asked Xuseen, who deeply sympathized with Jamaad's plight, to deliver the message of acceptance, and since poets could say with impunity what others could not, Xuseen was able to make it clear that the consent was given under duress. After he had heard the poem, Nuux magnanimously gave up his claim to Jamaad and married one of the Sayid's granddaughters instead.

The poet begins by telling the well-known story of the Lion's Share.

Said Lord Lion to Hyena, "Apportion the meat!"
Answered he, "Then your share is one half and no more -
Are we not a whole tribe, the rest of us here?"
The Mighty One's wrath at these words was great,
And raising his paw, with a powerful swipe
He knocked Hyena's eye right out.
The Foul-Faced One screwed up his snout
As the gory fluid spurted forth,
And whining and whimpering, with heavy feet,
Half-dead, he dragged himself away.

Then Jackal had to take his turn -
He shook with fear at the gnashing of teeth
As vengeful Lion caught hold of him fast
And commanded, "Now, Small-Paws, do your best!"
"O Dearest Uncle!" answered he,

"Take half of the meat and one third more,
Take breast and ribs, the lean and the fat,
And all the flesh from the chest and the hump -
O Chief, take all of it - it's all for you!"

The other beasts were left with no share
And they seized the Squirrel-Footed One -
"Jackal," they cried, "Lion is leader, that's true,
But he nevertheless has no tribe of his own.
Why should we who are many, a nation indeed,
Be cheated like this of our midday meal?"

"Why? Because of that sight just now
At the place from which Hyena crawled!
The words 'one half is your share and no more'
Were what brought down the Small-Rumped One.
That elder, once the proudest of us all,
Was struck down through foolhardiness,
So then there was left just me alone
To take up the burden of the task.
Now I, like you, must wait for my food
From the bountiful will of God the Master.
Could I, who am weak, have survived such a blow?
I feared for my life - am I therefore to blame
For this loss which all of us here are suffering?"

The poet turns to the matter of the marriage.

Apportioning meat at a lion's behest -
That is the task you have set me here.
My heart protests at the doing of a deed
For which folk will turn round and laugh at me.
O what a calamity has fallen to my lot!
I sought from you nothing - asked for no wealth
But still you brought distress on me.
I have lost the glory of my Brotherhood
And am deprived of my rank that was once so high.
Of all the excellent women whom once we had
We were left with only Jamaad and Naado.
Naado, who is the comelier of the two,

Disports herself now with Cali -
See, there she is, perfuming herself with incense smoke
As she makes herself ready for manly attentions!
There remains but one of all whom once we had,
But so be it - take Jamaad for yourselves as well!

ISMAACIIL MIRE

c.1860-1951. He was a member of the high command of the Dervishes during their war
against the foreign powers on Somali soil (1900-1920) and a close friend and adviser of
their leader, Maxamed Cabdille Xasan. During his service he composed poems committed to
the Dervish cause but after their defeat and a short period of imprisonment by the British
he returned to the pastoralist way of life and in his poetry concentrated on family and
neighbourhood concerns and on philosophical and religious reflection.

Change of Command

*The poet, who commanded the outlying fort of Shimbabiris, addresses his successor after he
himself had been recalled to headquarters by his leader, whom he calls "the Master".*

Listen to these words, Warsame Baarqab, before we part!
My skin flask is ready, filled with camel's milk and water,
For I am leaving, I and half the men,
And I shall mount Badow, my young mare,
When we glimpse the first faint light of dawn.
Tomorrow a long journey begins for us,
Along a road that will be full of dust,
Our destination the courtyard where the Master dwells.
For ten months now I have been away from him,
But from the house at Headquarters I have had good news.
Now indeed my heart is recovering,
For it was dry, like skin that is parched and thirsts for oil.

May you all be safe from the enemy's baleful malice,
From evil fortune and from outrage!
Be ever mindful of God's Word and of the Holy Law,
Hold fast to our accomplished Master
And cleave to the blessings of religion.

Many patrols and sentries must be set -
Vigilance above all is what I urge on you.
Slackness and faintheartedness - these you must shun,
Just as do those kingly men now garrisoned at Ayl.

A Hoopoe Rebuked

Composed in a year of great drought, when the spring rains, which are normally presaged by the cries of the hoopoe, had failed.

O Hoopoe, when you shed those tears,
Crying for the rains of spring
And spurning the lightest wink of sleep
Just because your craw is empty,
Do you imagine that you, and you alone
Are scorched by this dry season of *jiilaal*?

No, a great disaster has befallen
All God's servants, every one of them -
A drought is come that leaves nothing in its wake,
Just like the one that men called the Stalker.
Can it be right, then, to air your grievance
As if the suffering were yours alone?

Listen, O Hoopoe, to my tidings,
For I am an elder, grown grey-haired with experience.
There are camels, once the strongest of the herd,
That now look spare and gaunt -
There are men, once rich with milch-beasts,
Who are now too weak to rise at the assembly-ground.
Young men drift to the village, loitering, looking about -
In the shops there are dates, and guard must be kept
For they would take those dates and run
But for their fear of the tin-roofed jail.
The ostrich hen no longer stirs,
Nor half the asses of the wilderness.
In vain do the brawny-shouldered oryx bucks
Strive to raise themselves up from the ground -
Those solitary grazers sink down in the burnt scrubland.
A scant few gazelles among *garanuug* and *deero* survive
But for the tiny *sakaaro* and her fawns there is no chance.
The kudu is slaughtered, his flesh cut up for meat
Even by nobly-born men and soldiers in full array.
Never does the lion of the rocks now roar on Toomo plain
And the leopards that once were killers of goats

Have perished themselves at the hands of hunters -
Their cubs miaul no more from their cavern lairs,
For the men who buy skins have brought disaster on them.

Gone are the burden camels, gone are all the short-horned cattle
Sheep and goats, fattened for slaughter, are scarcely to be seen.
The skin flask from which the ghee was served
Is shrivelled and musty from disuse,
For want of oil the hair of goodly wives
Is now so brittle that it splits and falls.

Look, O Hoopoe, at those shining shapes
You see around you on the ground -
They are the bones of hyenas, bones of vultures, even.
Men like Maxamuud Garaad and Garaad Faarax
Have lost the horses they once owned.
In the vale that used to yield fine grazing
No beasts now bellow.
Thirst-stricken folk are dying in Garoowe and Bookh,
Exhausted, their bodies pricked by *gocondho* thorns.
They have no grain, but what would it avail them?
The water to boil it in is nowhere to be found.
The ill-omened bustard and his mate
Are fearful for their lives
And raise their boding cries of lamentation.

See, a band of men has been despatched
Against the locusts that live here in this land.
Soldiers in trucks appear from every side,
Poison is scattered on the grass
And there is death abounding.
But had those locusts done anything
To bring this fate upon themselves?
No, a decision was made one day to kill them, that was all.

So, Hoopoe, stop your wailing and your moaning
Or you may soon be hunted in your turn -
Stay quiet, speak softly, and you may yet escape arrest!

Listen, O Truck

The poet had received the news that his beloved nephew, Maxamed, was stricken with smallpox. When he saw a truck departing for the town where he lived he recited this poem.

Listen, O Truck, you who are almost ready to depart -
When all the goods are piled up on your back
And the travellers who want to go your way
Have been given their places right on top,
Then the lad who knows how to make you run
Will climb up on your neck
And four-gallon cans packed full of wares
Will be lashed to your flanks and ribs.
If you are steered quite straight
And driven without swerving from side to side
No ambling gait is yours -
Once a finger touches your starter
And the engine begins its humming,
Then off you move, direct to your destination
As if you were shot from a sling.

With your wheels and your hubs all covered in dust
You keep to the high road, grunting and groaning,
Until in a street you are brought to a stop.
Then at the place where you have parked
A cluster of people will gather round,
And if among them there is any man
Who has seen Maxamed, the handsome one,
Let him deliver my message to him -
Or if among the travellers I have any kinsmen,
Whether by marriage or by blood,
Let them convey this call.

As I lay on my mat of skins I was full of care
For the news that had come about Maxamed
Pressed heavily on my chest -
I had no solace, even, from the milk I drank
From Waaris, my cow that had just calved.

O God, Maxamed's mother is my sister!
O God, you who are the Only One,
Do not take him away from my very heart -
O God, do not block the road
By which comes help as nourishing as milk -
O God, do not bring me a letter bearing words of woe!

O God, I cannot spare Maxamed -
I could no more do without him
Than I could without my liver.
O God, to me he is the feet I walk on, he is my head
O God, he is the heart that beats inside me, and my right hand
O God, he is the hips that lift me and my long limb-bones
O God, he is my short ribs and the tendons of my spine!

Fleeting   Joys

Downpours of rain, dry valleys newly watered,
Hillsides resplendent with new verdant growth
And clans assembling under an acacia tree -
On such things were my thoughts and my affections set,
But this world provides no lasting satisfaction.

Meat of gelded camel being offered to the family,
Soured camel's milk, and food that does not spoil
Set out on massive dishes under handsome covers,
A bridal hut, with inner chambers specially contrived,
A straight-limbed girl with necklace and silk dress,
A young and splendid wife who passes to and fro
As she diligently serves you with your food,
Ever loth to leave you with your appetite unsated.
From her perfumed dress the scent of incense rises -
Truly her beauty was bestowed on her by God!
On such things were my thoughts and my affections set,
But this world provides no lasting satisfaction.

Burden camels, powerful and broad-necked,
Gelded camels, fit for the largest loads,

Great herds of camels, herds of cattle,
Weapons as numberless as grains of sand,
Girls deftly peeling fibre from the *qabo* bush
To make a great bowl to hold skimmed milk.
On. such things were my thoughts and my affections set,
But this world provides no lasting satisfaction.

A dish of choicest camel meat,
A sheep's quarter seasoned well with salt,
A wicker-framed milk vessel filled to the brim,
Tea and a drink of thinned-down honey,
Mutton spiced and finely sliced -
On such things were my thoughts and my affections set,
But this world provides no lasting satisfaction.

Ina Qooqan, Looshane, Qaabil, Tuure and Qadow Calameed -
These were my battle-horses, and Qalas, too -
On these I rode as we made ready for the holy war.
I accustomed myself to desert life
Often I hunted our enemies at the forest's edge
Often indeed I killed them and came back in triumph,
Adorned with the feather that the victor wears.
Many a time I was commander of our military ventures
And the forces of the infidels grew weary with me.
O how often have I sought to pursue the path of goodness!
And as for my transgressions -
Well, it is customary to stay silent.

But life does not last forever
And death reaches every living man.
I wander now in lonely places, my beard grown grey.
The world deceives that man
Who has not learnt the Words of Faith,
So instruct me in the Koran, O Teacher,
And let me tether a young she-camel as your reward!

What Will Come Next?

No longer do men who are bound together by ties of birth
Feel for each other the compassion and sympathy of old
And between two brothers born from one mother's womb
Loyalty no longer holds.
O Everlasting God, what will come next?
This must be the last era of the world!

In ill-famed houses girls are led into sin
And something even more disgraceful happens -
They are made to pay for their keep themselves.
O Everlasting God, what will come next?
This must be the last era of the world!

Foals are abandoned to growling hyenas
And left for the birds of prey to eat.
Donkeys are put into shelter at night
While splendid horses suffer neglect.
Base-born folk make arrogant clamour
While men of quality are degraded and poor.
O Everlasting God, what will come next?
This must be the last era of the world!

Wives reject their husbands, they refuse to stay at home -
Off they all go in pursuit of money from other men.
O Everlasting God, what will come next?
This must be the last era of the world!

This morning I sent out for provisions
But the errand was of no avail
For the money I had given was not enough
To buy even a slice of goat or mutton,
Or to fill a small measuring tin with food.
O Everlasting God, what will come next?
This must be the last era of the world!

Men sprang from Eve and from the seed of Prophet Adam,
And those among them who were born to be of noble rank

Would not now be suffering banishment from the world
If there were any real goodness in it still
And we were left to enjoy it for evermore in peace.
It is only a fool or a dim-wit who does not see
That this is clearly the last era of the world
And the time of the Trumpet of Doom is near.
O God, when that time comes
Do not throw us into the chastising flames
That burn in the Sevenfold Hell!

SAAHID QAMAAN

A pastoralist and political spokesman of his clan who died about 1930.

Equality

In some parts of Somalia the sultan of a clan was elected by an assembly and had powers that were circumscribed by customary law. A young sultan of the poet's clan abused this system by his dictatorial behaviour, and disastrously mismanaged the conduct of war with another clan. At the assembly which met to depose him, each section of the clan chose its best poet as spokesman and Saahid Qamaan was one of these; he starts by addressing another, Dubbad. The Maxamed mentioned later in the poem is probably Sayid Maxamed Cabdille Xasan, another leader whose misfortunes were popularly attributed to his misjudgment and tyrannical ways.

I have not composed poetry for many a day, Dubbad,
Not since the defeat we suffered at Sirawe -
The Battle-that-Severed-Men's-Feet
Was what it came to be called.
All turned to darkness for me at that time
And I launched no more of my poetic onslaughts,
But if I have a mind to I can still create a poem.

You who are discerning in speech and a man of wisdom,
Listen to these lines!
They came to me last night when I suddenly awoke,
And they concern a matter well-known to all the world -
A matter of slaughter, for we were slaughtered indeed
Because of that assembly where surely the jinns held sway!
Now men are asking themselves what will happen
Just as they did when Maxamed was the cause of their concern.
Have I not kindled a flame with these lines already
As if I were twirling a stick in a fire-drill?
Have I not set them out with clarity, as a teacher does
So that all may understand?

There is a matter concerning young men -
Young men who have lost all sense.

It is sweet indeed to receive tribute on first becoming sultan,
And a man of discretion may rightfully enjoy the benefits,
But he who spikes holes in a candelabra tree
Will regret his deed when he passes beneath its branches,
For the stinging sap that oozes from the cuts
Will peel his skin wherever it chances to drop.

Mark this -
A ranting tirade will not secure what you demand
If reason and forbearance have been of no avail -
A Muslim will never be enslaved
Even if beheading is to be his lot -
No man should destroy the flood-ditch dug around his homestead -
No vessel can hold more than the measure that is proper to it.

There is a matter concerning myself,
Something that affects me closely.
In the harshest time of the rainless season
When the grass of the pastures is sparse and dry
And men come with their herds to a deep-dug well,
Those clansmen who work together
Will each get a proper share in its use.
But if I am not given even a mouthful of water from the well,
Or if my tongue cannot lick so much as would cover a finger-tip
Of the honey I am asked to measure out abundantly to others,
Or if I must stand and offer greetings and assurances of fealty,
Or take up arms to defend privileges I myself am not accorded -
What then? I swear a triple oath by God -
Never shall I be treated thus!

I learned from my father, astute as a serpent
And from Magan, his forefather,
How to deal with my fellow-men.
I learned how to show them due respect
And I learned the duties that clansmen owe each other
For no matter what special talent I might possess
Are we not equals, all of us?

Degradation is something I utterly reject!
I shall not proffer my hand in greeting
To a man who will not give me a sleeping-mat
When I come to him as a guest -
I shall have no truck with a man
Who seems to set no value on my services!

QAMAAN BULXAN

A pastoralist who is said by the collector and editor of his poems (see Appendix V) to have been born in 1857 and assassinated in 1928. He played an important role in local politics as a spokesman and poetic champion of his clan.

The Stolen Wife

When the poet's young wife went to visit her kinsfolk a plot was hatched by them to provide spurious grounds for her to be divorced and to marry her to another man of their choice. The news of this treachery reached the poet when he came as a guest to the encampment of his friend Haybe.

It is only right, O Haybe,
That I should stoop down low with sorrow.
Do not lead me to my bed,
For there I toss from side to side
And wait in vain for sleep to come.

If someone is told that the girl he wed
Has been given in marriage to another man,
And if a broad javelin, poison-tipped,
Has deeply pierced his flesh right to its core,
Are these not grounds enough to be bereft of sleep?
I am such a man - don't lead me to my bed.

Once some cattle drank a water-hole quite dry -
Not even enough to fill a pitcher did they leave -
Yet back they came to it, looking for more.
I am like them - don't lead me to my bed.

It is said that a man once lost his mare
And followed her footprints, but found her dead.
He turned away from the tracks she had made
And setting off once more he roamed in circles
Around the place where her head was lying,
Hoping that somehow he would find her still alive.
I am like him - don't lead me to my bed.

A man beneath whose ribs consumption has forced its way
And filled his chest with putrid matter,
Will turn on his side in search of fitful sleep,
Unable to rid himself of sore resentment.
Food he still may take
But he knows for certain he will die.
I am like him - don't lead me to my bed!

In Praise of Barni Sheekh

Among all the women to be seen at Qorraxey -
Those who dwell in the heart of the town
And those who dwell in the countryside around,
The splendid wives and mothers,
The no-longer wives, divorced long since,
The slips of girls with combed-up topknots,
The maidens sedate and sturdy, the strapping wenches -
Take them one and all together,
And it is Barni Sheekh who excels in beauty!

Fair of skin, her gums the colour of the deep dark sea,
She has the aspect of a crescent moon.
With her glistening curls and her date-brown hue
She is as lustrous as a pearl.
So tall is her stature, so upright her bearing,
That you think you see a camelopard
If you glimpse her from afar.
There is strength in the build of her body
And she walks along at an easy pace,
Her left arm swinging in a graceful rhythm
That imparts beauty to her every step.

When you behold her dignified deportment,
When you feel the yearning that her character inspires
And discover the elegant beauty that God implanted in her,
Then your eyes will never cease their gazing.
The world is vast indeed
But however wide you may have roamed,

No matter what far land you may have seen,
In what country have you ever had news
Of a girl like Barni Sheekh?

NUUR UGAAS ROOBLE

A clan chief who died at the beginning of the 20th century.

Dissimulation

If any man intended aught of villainy against me
By God, how snug I made my forecourt for his bed-mat, none the less!
And if, with aggression in his thoughts
He pastured his horses to get them battle-fit,
How in spite of this I made him griddle-cakes of maize to eat!

Amiably I conversed with him for whom my body felt revulsion.
I did not hurry, I was patient in dealing with his tricks.
I showed a relaxed and easy mien,
My looks gave no grounds for suspicion in his mind -
Lips open, words betraying nothing of deceit, smiles,
Laughter on the surface, not rising from the gullet's depth.
In our game of *shax* I would make this move and that
And say, "This seems to be the one that's more to my advantage."
I offered banter and engaged in well-turned talk,
All the while setting a trap for him
Ready for the day when he would show his real intentions.
I would flood him with deceit, while I arranged my plan of action.

Then, when he was all unknowing and unwarned,
O how I struck him down!

CILMI BOWNDHERI

c.1910-1941. He spent his youth as a pastoralist but around 1930 he moved to the town of Berbera and worked as a baker. He fell in love with a girl called Hodon whom he hardly knew, and when it proved impossible to marry her he recited many desperate poems which won him nationwide fame. Hodon was given in marriage to another man and Cilmi is said to have died of grief. His grave in Berbera is sometimes visited by ill-starred lovers.

A Vain Love

When the camels come back thirsty
From many nights of grazing in the Hawd,
They are brought to a halt just short of the well
While a youth sings, trying to keep them calm.
But they want to press forward, for already they hear
The "hoobay! hoobay!" of the watering-chant.

I am like that when I hear you say "Hodon"!
Her name seems to you so simple
But to me it brings grief and woe.
I shall never give her up,
Not till the day they tread earth into her grave.

Rapt in a deceitful trance
I thought I was sleeping by her side,
But it was a jinn, not she herself,
A jinn made in the image of her sister.
I tried to catch her by the hand
But the place by my side was empty -
I found I was striving in vain
For there was no one there.
I tossed from side to side, then suddenly awoke -
I rumpled my bed like a prowling lion,
I attacked the bedclothes and pounded them,
As if it were they that had caused my loss.

Like a hero against whom men have combined
I covered my face, all but my defiant eyes.

I was humbled, like a boy who could not save from robbers
The herd entrusted to his care.
I felt disgraced, as a woman does
When the words "I divorce you" are said to her.

It is degrading to yearn for what you cannot have.
Alas, alas, what a disaster has befallen me!

A Vision

At times I made light of it
And I was free.
Then suddenly I was shown her in a vision
And she was radiant in hue, like a lighted lantern.
Surely she must have been imprinted on my heart
How else could I be so intoxicated with her?
Inside my breast she tick-tocks to me like a watch
At night when I sleep she comes to sport with me
But at early dawn she leaves
And turns into a rising pillar of dust.

The Messenger

Winds that possess the power of speech
Are something new in this world, perhaps,
But you must swear to me, O Wind, by the Everlasting One
That you will receive the impress of my words!

Indeed I would have gone to the sailing ships
And handed them my letters in a packet
But ships may tarry on their journeys
And nights may pass before they come to port,
So it is you, O Wind, whom I have chosen,
You who have the speed that I demand.
Swear to me then by the Everlasting One
That you will receive the impress of my words!
You pass above the ground,

Above the settlements of men,
Never resting, you run and run
As if sent by God on everlasting errands.
Weariness is not for you,
It is only the living whose breath gives out.
I have heard that other men have stepped forward
To claim the girl on whom my mind was set -
Wind, swear to me by the Everlasting One
That you will carry my words through the air!

Daaroole is where I found my solace,
That is the place that you must find,
And nothing must stop you -
Not bad roads, nor screens of matting.
Muuse knows the country well
And he knows where she is to be found.
There is a man who looks at her admiringly -
O this world is a precipitous mountain path!

Tell her that stone houses and walls would have felt the pain
Tell her that termite hills would have sprouted green grass
If they had but heard these words of mine!

FAARAX SHUURIYE

A pastoralist who died in the 1960s.

A Chief Is Thanked for the Gift of a Horse

Can one compare
    A man who puts his faith in prayers
    And is well versed in the rules that govern them,
    A man who turns to God, his body bowed,
    And kneels down, touching head to ground -
        With a dusty-footed apostate who shuns
        The cleansing that would make him pure for prayers?

Can one compare
    A man who knows the proper way
    To perform the tasks of voluntary prayer
    And in order to fulfil them tarries in the mosque,
    Telling his beads the while -
        With a disreputable blackguard?

Can one compare
    A man who observes Ramadan with faith,
    Fasting through all its thirty days,
    Taking no food from dawn to dusk -
        With a man in an eating-house,
        Forever munching pieces of bread?

Can one compare
    A man who sits atop a truck
    And, free from fatigue, rides fast to town -
        With a man who has to walk there,
        Marking the way with his footprints?

Can one compare
    A man who need not trudge about on foot
    For he rides a fine and steady horse,
    His feet forever in the stirrups
    His knees forever at its flanks -
        With a man who on a donkey
        Slowly makes his ungainly way?

Can one compare
    A man of resource, with ideas aplenty,
    On whom God has bestowed the virtues
    That might be found in a whole band of souls -
        With a sneering weakling who spoils the work of others
        And knows nothing of what it is that makes real men?

Can one compare
    A man who sets on a burly camel its full load
    And on top a canopied seat as well,
    And as the beast swings into its marching gait
    Listens to it noisily chewing the cud -
        With a man who puts two meagre packs,
        Weighing perhaps a quarter-pound apiece,
        On a badly trained and useless camel
        That again and again throws down its load?

Can one compare
    A man in whose home God places
    A helpmeet of true excellence,
    A wife who brings him contentment
    And is one of the houris of this world -
        With a man who has mistaken an evil-natured shrew
        For a woman who might bring him comfort and joy,
        But who is plagued and molested now instead?

Can one compare
 Me - a man who has composed countless poems with fluent ease,
 Me - a man who has come forth adorned with a feather of victory
 From many a set-to and skirmish carried on in verse,
 Me - a man whose words resound like rifle-shots -
  With a man who gets on his feet in the assembly-ground
  And bellows and blethers about nothing at all?

Can one compare
 This chief here, who has benefited Muslims as rain does the land,
 And from whom you can expect a gift
 Of a thousand rupees or a thousand riyals
 Or a swift-running horse or choicest camels -
 A gift he will bestow with as much ease
 As if it were worth less than my tooth-brushing stick,
 Or a mere four ounces of merchandise -
  With a niggardly miser?

Somalis are not good at judging the true value of men,
But now, setting my sights on truth,
I say before God that our chief is a true Muslim!
May his life be long - O God, grant this to him
And to his family, retinue and clan -
Let them nowhere be crushed by any disaster!

CUMAR XUSEEN 'OSTREELIYA'

He spent his youth as a pastoralist and most of his adult life as a seaman.   After his retirement he returned to the pastoral way of life and died in the 1960s at a very advanced age.   He was well known for his stories about his world-wide travels and adventures and had been particularly impressed by Australia where he spent some time ashore.   He spoke about it so much that he was given the nickname "Ostreeliya".

Where True Profit Lies

In the dry season the young men take most of the camels to distant wells and grazing-grounds, so that the areas nearer the family encampment do not become over-grazed. The people left behind rely for milk on the remaining camels, while water i s brought by camel caravan from the nearer wells.

When I turn my mind to the fibres of poetry, Maxamed, to their very core,
My sound-matching words have never failed to create a worthy heritage.
Even in my childhood I had already learnt the art of their composition
And tonight, when my beard is tinged with grey and covers even my
       cheeks,
I would be disgraced if my words were to be mismatched and lose their
      balance.
Listen to me then, for I am wont to make verses with consummate skill!

The care of sheep and goats - that's work for women and their children
And though there's glistening milk and buttermilk in plenty
When the fresh grass sprouts in the *karan* rains,
It's just enough for daily household needs, no more.
And as for cows - the milk from their udders is frothy and fresh
While you stay near water and the ground is bedecked with dew,
But when drought comes, horned beasts will perish, that is certain.
O you who tend ewes!
Remember, it's in camel-rearing that true profit lies.

A man distressed and hungry in the cold of the rainless season
Has only to taste the milk that issues, faintly sour,
From the udders of a camel
For him soon to feel there is a place deep in his body
Which has received comfort and solace.

72

As you drink it your body becomes moist, suffused with sweat -
O you who tend ewes!
Remember, it's in camel-rearing that true profit lies.

The she-camels may have stayed for months in the Hawd bushland ,
They may have fed only on *suud* acacia pods and winding *meygaag* plants,
Yet here they are, each one in calf, each beautiful and thriving!
Their delivery time is near, their bellies so big that they can hardly walk.
They do not hide their craving for salt, they long for brackish water.
The young men tending them herd them together along the road
And after a journey lasting days and nights they come to Dhamal
And stay there for a day on a patch of land, chewing at the salty soil.
Crystals of dried urine fall into the milk
That at night is pressed from their udders.
O you who tend ewes!
Remember, it's in camel-rearing that true profit lies.

When the call to prayers resounds at dawn
The camels throng at the thorny gate of their pen.
Two herdsmen set the young men to their tasks,
Allotting them work at the well or some other charge.
As soon as the walled pathway to the water-troughs
Has been strengthened with stones and stakes
The camels press through it, one by one,
Each as fleet as a horse that bears an important message,
And as they get near the water they utter cries of longing.
The men at the well give heed to the cries
And run to the ground they have swept clean in readiness.
The milch-camels now need wait no longer
After the hard time they have spent without salty water.
The herdsmen bring them quickly to the troughs,
Those with abundant milk and those who now have but little,
Those who have lately calved,
And the stud-beast, too, his hind legs stained with urine.
Carefree men are stationed there to sing for them,
Young men, their hair crimped with powdered clay,
Are set to the task of bringing each group to water in its turn.
Loudly they shout, like singers of the *dhaanto* dance song,
And swiftly the milking-vessels are passed around.

The camels now have had their fill
And on a grassy spot they are made to rest.
They move on then, like a water caravan
For which thirsty men are waiting.
They are driven on their way,
Back to the place from whence they came,
Stopping once again in the pens that were built for them
On an earlier journey they had made to water.
In truth, a man who drinks their milk that night
Will find that thorns will emerge from his flesh
That had been deeply embedded since childhood days!
O you who tend ewes!
Remember, it's in camel-rearing that true profit lies.

The camels continue on their homeward way
Until Idhaamo has been left behind,
Then pens are made for them on grassy ground.
Branches are spread to serve as awnings
Over those that have lately given birth -
The skin of their foals seems like finest silk!
Thunder resounds as the spring cloud pours down rain
And now the herdsmen can build their pens
On the homeward side of the Hawd's borders.

There is no true nourishment to be found
In glinting town-bought milk, nor yet in rice,
But when the camels come home to the family encampment,
To people worn out by the rainless season of *jiilaal*,
Then can vessels which had grown musty with disuse
Be filled again with good sour milk.

A Somali may gather great wealth,
Diamonds he may have and houses too,
He may even wear clothes of wool or fine white cloth
And sport a splendid turban -
But he has no legacy to leave behind him
Unless he rears the beasts whose necks bear wooden bells.

My commendations are not complete by any means
Nor has my praise been lavish
And if I were to illumine camels a little
And cast more light on their true qualities,
No one would ever wish to sell the females of the herd,
No one would ever give them away,
No one would offer them even as prisoners' ransoms.
God placed them on this desolate land
Like living stones chipped from a rock -
For if they had not come from a rock
Would men invoke them in their oaths?
The three who go together - suckling, dam and foster-dam -
Are as the sinews of your spine to you.
There are losses to which men can resign themselves,
But no man will ever submit to the loss of his camels.
O you who tend ewes!
Remember, it's in camel-rearing that true profit lies.

The poet remembers how he took part in camel-raids in his youth :

Firearms were aimed, one against the other, and bullets flew
Hissing like drops of urine shed by evil jinns
And guns killed warriors as tall and fine as trees.
Many a time, rifle in hand, I approached the object of my desire.
In the midst of the struggle there I was,
Bent on carrying off the females of the herd!

Call the camels!   Call the camels!
A man who has reared no camels will always be a pauper!

In Praise of Weris

*It was the custom that when a man was seeking a girl in marriage, and her family looked on
him with favour, he would pay a visit to her homestead, bringing gifts.   With him would
come some of his kinsmen, to add solemnity to the visit and to protect him, and the gifts, on
the journey.   In his youth Cumar Ostreeliya accompanied his cousin Maxamed on such a
journey to the home of Weris, Maxamed's bride-to-be, and he composed this poem in her
honour.*

If in these verses, linked by the sound of "S"
I were to give a true account, O Weris, of your qualities,
Unlocking the coffers of my skill
And opening my breast where clocklike beats my heart,
And were I to describe your appearance
Just as it was first created -
Why, the men who dwell in distant Sirow
Would all come here to seek you out!
But since the evil eye of jealousy
Is not wont to miss its aim,
I shall instead speak simply.

Listen, then, to my words tonight,
For this is no time to sleep -
See, we have brought fire and pulled aside
The barrier gate of the thorny fence!

* * * * * * *

It was for your sake, Weris,
That my body was scorched and thirsty in the waterless plain,
That Maxamed's skin was burnt in the sun's fierce heat,
That our backs were torn by the belts and bandoliers we wore!
Time and again we barely survived the dangers we had to meet
From hostile warriors, from spies who roamed the land,
From the silent-footed lion -
All for your sake, Weris!

For you we had picked out horses, powerful geldings,
Then from among the camels we chose some females
And threesomes of suckling, dam and foster-dam

And more young females not yet mated.
If we are such men as this,
Then the sheer love you must feel for us
Will surely make you abjure your food!

I have not botched these verses -
Have I not steered them along the proper path?
Men who have not learnt to compose verses linked by "S"
Will digress and lose their way
But I - have I not linked them like a chain
That was made by an Indian goldsmith?
I have more to speak in praise of Weris,
Words which I warrant to be true.

In our party there are Cismaan and Jibriil,
The finest ribs of the Jaamac family,
Young men fashioned by God to be of equal stature
Who are like the tall *siiq* trees by the river -
Elegance has been our lot, and the gift of nobility!
Eight cousins we are, armed with Martini rifles
And bringing two bundles of dates wrapped up in fibre mats
And rolls of silk protected well with skins.
Here at her people's encampment we had been expected,
And a courtyard screened from sweeping winds was given us
With a well-sheltered place to stack our firearms.
We have been offered the guest food proper for marriage-kin -
Dishes of cooked grain, sour camel's milk, ghee in a painted bowl -
But our eyes are for her and her alone
As the man brings in the food and carries it away again.

We are overcome as we look at her.
Her body is as erect, it seems to us,
As a ladder standing upright.
They have adorned her with jingling armbands
And an amber necklace has been placed around her throat.
A long dress covers all her form,
And a shawl of calico, brought from Berbera,
Allows nothing to be seen but her eyes.
A striped shift of many colours

Enhances the beauty of her apparel.

Her sandals, solidly-soled and finely-balanced,
Are cut from the finest cow-flank leather.
As she passes along an encampment lane
The clatter of her jewels
Makes the sound of bullets or a cracking whip.
In salute we fire three times into the sky.
Then greetings are exchanged, and pleasant conversation.
The words a dimwit chooses come out garbled
But not so those of Weris -
Is it not true that by the age of nine
She had been taught to learn by heart
The lines of the Sacred Knowledge?

Her eyebrows are closely knit,
Her face suffused with radiance.
Both a pure body and a beauteous shape
Were given to her by God.
See how her hair is plaited,
Like the feathers of an ostrich cock
When he has folded them smoothly down!
A man who has gazed on her for even one hour
Will need no other joy until he enters Paradise.
Are her lips not outlined
As if they were drawn with charcoal ink?
O, they are such wonders!
See how the flying dust never settles upon her form -
Can it be that she is a kinswoman of the Turkish sultans
Or perhaps of the lords of Arabia?

O Weris, thanks to the pattern in which God shaped you,
And the wealth that your family possesses,
No woman is your peer,
You who appear as a lantern shining bright!

MUUSE XAAJI ISMAACIIL GALAAL

c. 1915-1980.   A prominent collector and devotee of Somali oral literature, traditions and starlore. He spent his youth as a pastoralist, then trained as a teacher. After independence he became a language and literature researcher in the Cultural Department of the Ministry of Education and later in the Academy of Arts and Sciences, and he played a pioneering role in the development of the official orthography which was introduced in 1972.   In 1956 his collection of traditional stories, (see Appendix V), had been published in London; this was the first work of its kind to be written in Somali by a Somali. "The Serpent" is a tale from this collection, earning its place in an anthology of poetry because of the verses with which he embellished it; the prose narrative is summarised here.   The poet originally couched the serpent's farewell speech in what might be called heightened prose, and we have presented it in the poetic lines into which it seemed to fall.

The   Serpent

There was once a soothsayer, skilled at foretelling the future by turning and counting his beads, who had such success with his predictions that his fame reached the sultan.   At an assembly the sultan ordered him to work out a horoscope for the coming year, promising him a rich reward if it came true but death if it did not.   With trepidation the soothsayer began to turn his beads, but time and again the result was meaningless, and the impatient sultan finally told him to come back in a week's time with his prediction - or die.

For six days the soothsayer wandered in the wilderness, counting over his beads, but not one intelligible answer came out, and he resigned himself to death. Suddenly he was startled by a serpent, and still more startled when it spoke to him with kind words.   They swore a mutual oath of peace, and the serpent offered to help him, asking only for a half-share in the sultan's reward as his payment. Eagerly the soothsayer agreed, and the snake began:

I have found out the secrets of the time that is to come
Listen to what I have to say!

Eight years have passed since the deeds of Ibliis, Prince of Evil.
The round of the years has brought back the jinns
And all their wicked deeds.
There are signs to be seen in the return of this eighth year -
A wife who covers her head with a mourning-scarf,
Brave men slaughtered, looted herds,
Vultures pecking at the flesh of sturdy warriors,
Disaster!
Men are preparing busily for war,

Their rusty battle-spears made newly sharp.
Horses are fattened, and harnessed ready for the fray,
And once-dry waterskins, with fastenings new-fixed,
Are ready again to slake men's thirst.
Whether you close your eyes in sleep, whether you flee,
Or whether in readiness you draw your sword from its scabbard,
Soon there will come a fierce and determined cohort
And against the very dust the encounter with them raises
You will cry out to God in awe!

Joyfully the soothsayer blessed the serpent and hurried off to tell the sultan that he must prepare for war. For the whole year there was fighting, but his people gained a final victory, and gratefully he bestowed on the soothsayer large herds of valuable animals.

As the soothsayer drove them away he remembered his promise that the serpent should get half the reward. But the animals were so beautiful - and he began to question the wisdom of keeping his promise. Would it not be more sensible to kill such a dangerous creature? He took up his sword and went in search of his benefactor - but the blow he aimed at it hit only the tree where it had been lying, while it slithered away to safety.

Now the time came when once again the sultan wanted to know what the next year would bring, and once again the soothsayer could get no answer from his beads. In despair he went back to the serpent, contrite and apologetic, and begged him with tears to help him. The magnanimous creature agreed, but had a few words to say first:

Mankind, O Diviner, was destined, it seems,
To be the cause of this world's woes.
Butchering each other was *your* invention
'Stab' was a word that *you* devised,
And the fire that you have kindled
Will consume a large part of creation.
When you are weak and defenceless
How fond you are of friendship
And the support of mutual aid -
But for the man you called your friend
When you were pressed by need,
You care nothing when your purpose is achieved!

You have broken the covenant into which you entered
And the pact that once was made between us.
The evil deeds of the sons of Adam
Will surely end by destroying the world!

What you say out loud with your lips
You do not really mean in your heart.

It was I who saved you from a trap
When you came to me in such dire straits.
I expected some reward from you
But instead, you dolt, the profit I gained
Was a deadly blow from a hilted sword!
The thud and crack of that sword of yours -
The cloud of dust that vexed my head -
The fear in which I fled from you -
Leaping, stumbling, dashing against euphorbia trees -
My ears were made deaf by all that happened!
O how I was taken in by you -
By that trickling tear, that gaunt aspect,
Those pleading words which touched my flesh,
Those jinn-like supplications!

So do not look for trust from me
For that trust fell down a very deep hole.
I shall tell you this, for the sake of God -
You are a doer of evil deeds!
I have no doubt that many a time
You have oppressed weak men and orphans,
And in my view you are paying now
For all the injustice you committed -
An old debt of yours is now being settled.

Nevertheless - tell the sultan who sent you here
That a wasting drought will come.
Tell him that grass in the pastures will wither,
That trees will die, the ones that stand in groves
And the ones that grow alone and tall.
Tell him that water will no longer flow
In pool or shallow well, valley or running stream.
Tell him that those who are weak and poor
Will perish with their flocks
And only the black-headed sheep
And the sturdiest camels will live.

But tell him, too, that hard work and resourcefulness
Will help a man to survive till the rains return.

The soothsayer was almost dazed with gratitude, and this time he assured the serpent that he
would bring him the whole of the reward that the sultan had promised him. The serpent only
replied, "Well, we shall see!"

Once again the prediction came true, but the sultan and his people, who had been forewarned
and had gathered stocks of food, came through the hard times while others perished.   The
soothsayer received his reward, and as he was driving his animals away, he remembered his
promise to give them all to the serpent.   But the love of wealth stirred in him, and he told
himself it would be foolish to give such beautiful animals away - he would keep them for
himself and not go near the serpent at all.

But a third time he was called by the sultan to predict the coming year, and a third time he
realised that there was nothing for it but to consult the serpent.   The creature laughed when
he saw him, but without rancour began his prediction:

Tell the sultan who sent you here
That the sky will bring back the clouds once more
For it is barren no longer, and carries the Dirir rains.
Tell him that soon, on a night half-spent,
Flashes of lightning will be seen,
And the bountiful plenty of the Daydo rains
Will fall, just as it used to do.
Tell him that showers will pass over the land
That had been laid bare by drought.
Tell him that the herds will suffer no more
On their long treks to the water-holes.
Tell him that torrents will scurry like lizards
Through the dry scrub of arid valleys,
That fresh grass will spring up round the encampments
And that among the herds that have survived the drought
There will be beasts in milk.

Tell him that the wife who was banished from her husband's side
In the rigorous months of the rainless season
Will soon build a hut as spacious as a house of stone.
Now she can put off her workaday clothes
And dress herself anew in the silks
She had kept rolled up against this time.
Incense-burners appear from nooks and crannies

And a mat for sleeping is spread in a snug recess,
For her husband had had no thought of love
While the harsh dry season lasted,
But now that his flesh has lost its gauntness
He will come once more inside the hut.
Now he can choose what food he will eat -
No longer is he driven by hunger alone.
Over and over, with tender little words, he will be asked
To take more, and yet again more.
His wife will come and go, fetching this bowl or that,
And as she passes to and fro so close to him
The love that had grown old will become young again,
And in their revelry and play sons of blessing
Will be conceived, sons bright as thunderbolts.

Tell the sultan, too, that the younger men
Will not remain for long unwed.
They will marry, in a befitting way,
The girls they have been yearning for,
And riding displays and dancing
Will entertain and honour them.
And tell him, finally, that a man who so wishes
Will be free to turn his mind to faith and prayer.

Everything befell as the serpent predicted, and the sultan and his people had a joyful year. The soothsayer, more than ever repentant of his treatment of the serpent, gathered all the animals together that he had received as reward and went in search of him. He offered them all to him, asked for his forgiveness, begged that they should become friends, and finally asked him, "You, who are wise, will you tell me about the world and about life?"

In answer the serpent said,

As for friendship - I become a friend to no one.
I either harm a man or help him,
According to the purpose for which I have been sent.

As for forgiveness - I have forgiven you.
As for the animals you brought to me -
I give them all back into your hands,
But nevertheless I regard the gift
As having been accepted.

Now as for the world and life - I tell you this:
World there is, but life is not distinct from it.
Your life, as you call it, goes as the world goes
For God made the world with many patterns
And it is these that rule men's lives.

When war is the pattern of the times
All men are at enmity with each other,
And thus it was that in the war just past
You took up your sword against me
Even after I had helped you,
And said to yourself, "Cut off his head!"
And then again, at a time of drought
No man is generous to his fellows,
So you ran away with all your herds,
Giving me no share in the sultan's reward.
But when there is a pattern of prosperity,
What man is ever niggardly or full of hate?
So you came to me, offering me all you had,
Not keeping even one animal for yourself.
Each time it was the pattern, not you yourself,
That forced you to do whatever you did.

And now I shall tell you who I am.
I am not a serpent, but Fate, the Leveller,
And you will not see me again after this day -
Farewell!

AXMED MAXAMED GOOD 'SHIMBIR'

A singer, musician and composer of lyrics who was active in the 1970s.

A Lover's Fears

Unless you are there within my sight
I crave no rest in sleep.
Wakeful, I cry aloud to you
As a young camel calls to its dam.

And just as a newly-orphaned suckling
Becomes tied by all the bonds of love
To the milch-camel which has fostered it,
So am I tied to you.

* * * * * * *

I made a vow
So fast to run
That winning I would gain you.
But faster still
A camel strode -
Loaded he was with curving poles -
He trod me down,
And fire flared all around me.

* * * * * * *

I dreamed, and you were there,
Your wedding-feast prepared -
O wait for me!
Give me your trust
And cast your gaze
On what lies deepest!

85

CALI SUGULLE

A well-known and popular playwright, poet, and actor whose career began in the 1950s.

A Happy Marriage

In this scene from a play, on the eve of their daughter's wedding Caateeye and his wife Cutiya remember their own life together.

CAATEEYE: Many a time we have been hungry,
Many a time we have suffered thirst,
Yet all in all we have not had bad luck.
Life is full of trouble, and it is short -
Short as a journey needing only one night's rest.
Often the fare we had was meagre
But were there not times as well
Of meat and milk in plenty?
And there were days and there were nights
That can never be forgotten.
You remember them, Cutiya, don't you?
And if God allows it
Other wonderful things like that
Are still in store for us.

CUTIYA: O Caateeye, one does not forget those nights and days!
That is what the bond between us -
That is what our first homecoming together -
Were all about!

CAATEEYE: Ah, how right she is!

CUTIYA: The rain-clouds that thundered, the lightning that flashed
And the sight on the horizon of the fresh grass they brought,
The wild fruit that ripened -
The *higlo* that put forth its berries
And the *hohob* that we picked together -
I have never forgotten these things,
I keep them in my mind, my bosom and my heart.

86

XASAN SHEEKH MUUMIN

A modern playwright, poet and singer; in 1968 the play from which this poem is taken achieved extraordinary popularity.

The Betrayed Girl

A girl has been deserted after being tricked into a bogus marriage.

Yesterday at dead of night, lamenting and calling
Like a suckling lioness who has lost her cubs,
Or like a mountain oryx whose body
Has been pierced by an arrow-point,
Again and again I stumbled down steep banks
But sought you all in vain.
You know what seared me - then judge it fairly,
For you it was who wronged me!

A man once owned great throngs of camels,
But one day, between noon and eventide,
A band of raiders came down among them -
And from that day his prosperity,
And the sour milk he used to drink,
Were gone, all gone.
Now he sits in an empty zariba,
His children hungry, his camel-calves orphaned -
And just like him I am ill with grief.
You know what seared me - then judge it fairly,
For you it was who wronged me!

The home we made, the bed I spread for you,
The trust between us, our oath and our resolve -
If you have turned away from all these things
And abandoned me in a wilderness
Then it was sheer folly that possessed me -
But avenging fate will find you without fail!
You know what seared me - then judge it fairly
For you it was who wronged me!

87

AXMED ISMAACIIL DIIRIYE 'QAASIM'

A modern poet who worked as a civil servant until his retirement.

Bitter and Sweet

Consider the aloe - how bitter is its taste!
Yet sometimes there wells up a sap so sweet
That it seems like honey in your mouth.
Side by side the sweet and bitter run
Just as they do, my friends, in me,
As I switch from sweet to bitter
And back to sweet again.

My two hands, right and left, are twins.
One twin gives food to strangers and to guests,
It sustains the weak and guides them.
But the other is a slashing, cutting knife -
As sharp to the taste as myrrh,
As bitter as the aloe.

Do not suppose I am the kind of man
Who walks along one path, and that path only.
I go one way, and seem a reasonable man,
I provoke no one, I have the best of natures -
I go another, and I'm obstinate and bold,
Striking out at others without cause.

Sometimes I seem a learned man of God
Who retreats in ascetic zeal to a secluded sanctuary -
I turn again and I'm a crazy libertine,
Sneakily snatching whatever I can get.

I am counted as one of the elders of the clan,
Esteemed for my wisdom, tact and skill in argument,
But within me there dwells a mere townee, too -
A no-good layabout he is, at that.

I'm a man whose gullet will allow no passage
For food that believers are forbidden to eat,
And yet I'm a pernicious, hardened thief -
The property of even the Prophet himself
Would not be safe from me.

I have my place among the holy saints,
I am one of the foremost of their leaders,
But at times I hold high rank in Satan's retinue,
And then my lords and masters are the jinns.

It's no good trying to weigh me up -
I can't be balanced on a pair of scales.
From this day to that my very colour changes -
Nay, I'm a man whose aspect alters
As morning turns to evening
And back once more to morning.

Muslims and infidels - I know their minds
And understand them through and through.
"He's ours!" the angels of Hell proclaim of me
"No, ours!" the angels of Heaven protest.

I have, then, all these striking qualities
Which no one can ignore -
But who can really know my mind?
Only a grey-head who has lived for many days
And learned to measure what men are worth.

And now, my friends, each man of you -
If either of the paths I follow
Takes your fancy and delights your heart,
Or even if you cannot bear to lose
The entertainment I provide,
Then come to me along that path -
You're free to make a choice!

MAXAMED IBRAAHIM 'HADRAAWI'

1943-. A very popular and prolific poet and playwright, who spent his childhood in a pastoralist environment but was educated in Aden, later becoming a student and then a teacher at the College of Education at Lafoole in Somalia. In 1973 he was imprisoned for composing poems whose symbolism was interpreted as being critical of the government. On his release five years later he was appointed Director of the Fine Arts Department of the Academy of Arts and Sciences, but in the same year he left his post to join the Somali National Movement, one of the rebel groups which brought down the government in 1991.

At the Grave of Cilmi Bowndheri

Cilmi Bowndheri was the poet (q.v.) who is said to have died of love for a girl called Hodon.

O my king among poets!
You who were driven onward to destruction
By your sorrows, by your helpless anger
And by the harshness meted out to you -
O Cilmi, you who died from passion's griefs,
You are the very paragon of love!
The perfection of the poet's art is in your lamentations -
Accept my greetings, praise and homage!

I know full well you are requited now
For all the pains you suffered in this world,
But there are some questions I would ask you.
Do you lodge in Paradise? Do you lie in fresh, cool shade?
Do you pick ripe fruit, and do the houris sing for you?
Do they grant whatever you may want of them?
Have you and Hodon beheld each other in the court of God?
Have you spoken to her and she to you?

But why should I be concerned with any of womankind?
How can I ever be at peace with them
Or exert myself unstintingly on their behalf?
For it was they, was it not, who tempted you away,
Beguiling you with a cloud that brought no rain
And a deceitful vision on the far horizon?
They who lured you to a dry and empty pool,

To a place that was swept by hot and noxious winds?
When you were thirsty it was they, was it not,
Who filled you with vain longings?
From their hands came suffering
And a robe of mourning.
They planted anguish in your flesh,
They stole away your sleep,
They enveloped you in darkness,
They cast you into a pit and covered you close,
They harried you to the top of a cliff
Only to hurl you headlong down.
Wounding you, they severed an artery,
And they struck you down on sandy ground
Throwing you into the dust.
You were abandoned in the wilderness
And there the hyenas and ravening beasts of prey
Gnawed at the flesh that clung to your bones
While scavenger crows and vultures
Pecked at the scraps that were left.

But my reflections on women must be tempered
Since it is of women, after all, that our mothers are born,
And the maternal breast will come to their aid,
Defending them against me, against my contentions
And against my manly pride.
If they had no such strong protection
Who would ever trouble about them?
Who would ever hunger after them?
Who would offer riches in exchange for them?
Who would bring them to their homesteads?
Who would even bother to talk to them?

* * * * * * *

But I was telling how I was inspired to visit Cilmi's grave,
To offer my homage, my salutations and my song.
It was my purpose to find out for sure his dwelling-place
And to know what wealth had been bestowed on him
When he arrived at last in the presence of God.

Then I asked him concerning Hodon, did I not?
To be sure, he has left for his eternal home,
But some links with this world he still must keep
That stretch, like telegraph wires, from here to there -
And I got my answer - was that not so?

For yesterday, as dusk began, I spied a hoopoe -
He who bears messages from the Other World -
And from afar, with nods and becks,
He signalled me to join him.
I was walking in the company of men,
So falling back, I sought him in his hidden haunt
And there I gathered all his news,
Prompting him now and again
With "Go on, then" and "Yes?"

The message that the hero sent me,
Entrusting it to the hoopoe's care, was this:
"Listen, you who sought me out
So zealously and questioned me,
I know it was your sympathy with my fate
That brought you to my grave in this wild land of scrub.
You offered me homage and called me from my resting-place,
You who yourself excel in the poetic art -
Here, then are my tidings!

"It is only on earth that troubles dwell,
Only there that folk suffer from thirst,
Only there that men of true mettle
Are treated disdainfully when they have no wealth.
It is there that fortune favours women,
It is there that women hold men in poor esteem!

"But now I live in Paradise,
Where full contentment is assured
To those who showed forbearance when on earth -
No disappointments await them in their graves!
In the past, my life held hardship and misfortune
But recompense is granted in this Other World.

I live here in a cool and shady homestead,
Sheltered by a cloud above my head,
Screened by thunder and lightning from the sun.

"I fill my water-pail from a pool that is ever full,
I linger beside clusters of ripe fruit
That gladden my eyes as I pick and eat
Like a child, whose mother is feeding him
Now from her right breast, now from her left -
Or like a suckling camel nourished by his dam.
No thought I give to Hodon or to love of her
For others have come to take her place.
Now there are houris to engage in amiable talk,
Houris who are commanded to sing for me
And who encompass me with the inner borders of their robes.

"But a herd of sturdy camels is thronging towards me now!
The water-pail is filled and ready - my task awaits me -
Farewell, my brother, farewell to you!"

Beledweyn

*The poet accompanied a troupe of actors to Beledweyn, a country town, where he met a girl
for whom he composed this mock-romantic poem.*

Love! May you live for evermore!
It can't be true - it's a lie, I say,
That it was you who killed Bowndheri!
Love! May you live for evermore!
It can't be true - it's a lie, I say,
That your piercing iron-hard thrust
To liver, heart or flank
Is a wound no physic can heal
Nor nursing mend - it can't be true!

When I went down to Beledweyn
The times were blest and prosperous.
The river had overtopped its banks
And bestowed its water on the farmlands,

Grass fit for grazing covered the ground
And trees and bushes were bedecked with blooms.
The maize and millet were threshed and winnowed
And the grapes were now all ripe.
There was a *bullo* dance, and others, too, -
People danced and danced till dawn's first light
As the homesteads rejoiced in the season of spring.

Now, in that town, on the eastern side,
There lives a queen!
Resplendent she is as sun-gilt water,
And the beauty and charm of womanhood
Are found in her to true perfection.
Her long hair falls as far as her heels -
I could compare it only with ostrich plumes -
And on the crown of her head there are auburn shades
Which evenly sweep to right and left.
Her locks are anointed with scented ghee
And they serve her even when she sleeps
For does not her body rest on them?
Are they not a pillow for her head?
Does she not spread them as a coverlet?

And when I met her -
Ah, what a fervent longing,
What joy she planted in me!

It was in the morning, early,
On the eighth day of the month,
In Beledweyn, halfway across the Swaying Bridge
That spans the water, swinging to and fro -
It was there we chanced upon each other,
Beerlula and I.
I stopped and spoke to her in greeting
And she returned me words of welcome.
We arranged to meet - it was fate -
She said, "Be here tomorrow!"
Didn't she?

"I can't face the journey home -
I'm desperately ill -
Please cancel the departure -
Consider the state I'm in!"
But the news of my affliction was not welcomed -
"We're off today!" was the troupe's response.
The director even thought that I was lying -
That harsh and wicked man ignored my plight
And didn't want to know about it, did he?
Then most of the troupe got on the truck -
Quite blatantly they did it -
They all climbed up from one side
And I had to climb up from the other.

When strong feelings get out of hand
And longings overpower the mind,
One prays sometimes for evil things to happen
And did I refrain from this? I didn't, no!
I prayed that some part inside that truck,
Some metal part, would cease to work,
I prayed that the petrol-tank would spring a leak,
I even prayed that the driver would get ill
And not recover before departure time.

At dawn, and through the first hot morning hours
Far on the horizon we could see a giant shape,
The massive tree that all Beledweyn knows as Baar.
The wind rushed through its withered pods -
We heard it calling out to us -
We heard it whistling, didn't we?

The truck went rocking on its way,
Back and forth and side to side,
And grievous illness gripped me again.
The evening heat rose towards me from the dunes
And I fainted.
Beerlula seemed to be at my side
A green meadow lay beneath our feet
The season was prosperous, the times propitious,

And together we danced the *beerrey* dance -
But now my senses returned to me
And what had it been but a deluding dream?

Like a bird of prey on the wing
The truck sped on and on
And climbed to the top of a lofty hill.
As I gazed around me,
Peering now to one side, now to the other,
It came into my mind to jump -
I cared nothing for the risk of death!

I am a man who has been bewitched
I long to be not here, but there -
Not in Banaadir, where I'm living now,
But in Beledweyn - that is where I want to be!
I look for her, I call her name - Beerlula!

O God - make Beledweyn a garden of solace and joy!
O God - make Beledweyn an abode of happiness!
O God - turn aside from Beerlula any threatening harm!
O God - let her live in peaceful and prosperous times!

APPENDICES

.

APPENDIX I

The Oral and the Written Medium

All the poems on pages **7-78** were composed, disseminated and preserved orally, that is entirely without recourse to writing. The poet's medium of communication was the recital, and the poems assumed written form only when they were taken down by collectors of oral literature. There could be, and often was, a gap of many years between the original composition and the writing down of the oral texts. The poets whose poems are given on pages **85-96** used writing as they worked on their poems, but the texts still reached the public originally through recitals, broadcasts or recordings, though publication might follow later. Between these two sections is the poem on pages **79-84**, which is exceptional in never having been disseminated orally, for it was edited from the poet's manuscript notes and then published.

The accurate transmission of an oral text across a long period of time was only possible because of the existence among Somalis of an unwritten copyright law. When a poet gave a public recital anyone was allowed to learn his poem by heart, but if the memorizer wished to recite that poem to another audience he was under a strict obligation to aim at verbatim memorization and to try his best to reproduce the text faithfully at each performance, for it was regarded as unethical to make wilful changes in the text. At each recital the name of the author had to be stated, and plagiarism by a reciter was, if detected by his audience, punished by ridicule and a severe loss of reputation. As Somali poems are never of epic length, accurate memorization was not too difficult to achieve.

APPENDIX II

Pronunciation of Somali words

In several of the poems I have had to leave a number of names of natural objects in the original Somali, having been unable even to identify, let alone find English equivalents for, some of the flora and fauna which is specifically Somali. These words, as well as proper names, are written in the official orthography, written in Latin characters, which was introduced in 1972, and as the pronunciation of a few of these characters is different from that of the same letters in English, a brief guide is given here. Only a very rough approximation to the pronunciation is aimed at; anyone who wishes to acquaint himself with Somali phonetics will find guidance in works on the language listed in Appendix IV.

The letter **c** is used for a vowel-like pharyngeal sound, similar to the 'ain' in Arabic, which is normally not heard by non-Somalis. It is this which is responsible for familiar Muslim names like Ali, Omar and Said appearing as **Cali, Cumar** and **Saciid** in Somali orthography.

The letter **x** very roughly corresponds to the English **h,** so that Hassan, Hussein and Mohamed become **Xasan, Xuseen** and **Maxamed** in Somali.

The single vowel letters **a**, **e**, **i**, **o** and **u** have approximately the same pronunciation values as in Spanish or Italian. When these letters are doubled they represent the same vowel sounds as the corresponding single letters but are longer; they never represent the sounds conventionally associated with the doubling of vowel letters in English as in 'keep' or 'book'. The letter **a** followed by **w** jointly represent a diphthong as in such English words as 'cow' or 'brow'.

The letter **s** is always pronounced as in the English word 'hiss', and **g** as in the English word 'go'.

In publications relating to Somalia which are written in European languages the reader will encounter a large variety of divergent spellings of Somali proper names. It should also be noted that some Somali proper names have optional pronunciation variants, e.g. **Cabdille** and **Cabdulle**, **Cabdiraxmaan** and **Cabduraxmaan**.

APPENDIX III

Alliteration and Scansion

In Somali poetry alliteration, not rhyme, is used for structural bonding and ornamentation and it follows the same matching rules as those followed by English poets before the Norman Conquest: consonants alliterate with identical consonants and all vowels are deemed to be alliterative with each other, irrespective of their quality. There is, however, one important difference between the two systems: while alliteration in Old English is normally confined to individual lines or small groups of lines, in Somali the same alliteration is sustained through the whole poem, even if it has as many as two hundred lines. How this 'all-through' alliteration operates can be seen from the first ten lines of the original version of the poem, 'Riposte to a young opponent in a poetic duel' by Raage Ugaas, which is translated in this anthology. The recurrent alliterative sound is the consonant **b**.

Baraar habarti loog ka ma furto gawrac kama baajo
Bil saddex ihi galabtii hadday beelo kaa bixiso
Beladkaad u jeeddiyo iftiin beelo ba ma geyso
In kastoo la baabuuniyoo baayac lagu doono
Bisinkiyo karaamada haddii loo buraanburiyo
Baal xuunsho beec iyo gorgoro beeso kuma gooyo
Baqal luga ka dheeree fardana beder ma gaarsiiyo
Baakuri tarkeed way bus kicin laba boqooloode
Burus-qayl biyiyo caanaba ma sido mana bukhuur daayo
Bahal raadki meel helay libaax baabushii mariyey

In addition to the formal constraint of alliteration, Somali poetry has a system of quantitative scansion reminiscent of that used in Ancient Greek. Its prosodic units are morae, i.e. time units measured by syllabic length; a short syllable counts as one mora and a long one as two. The length of a syllable in Somali scansion, unlike in Classical Greek, is measured by the length of vowels and diphthongs only. There are a number of poetic metres and each has its own rules concerning the number of morae, the distribution of short and long syllables and their division into feet. 'Riposte to a young opponent in a poetic duel'

103

is in a metre which is particularly favoured for poems of substance aimed at a wide audience. Each line in this metre has twenty morae, with the possiblity of an initial 'upbeat' mora, which is rare. The line is divided into four equal feet of five morae each. The sign ◡ represents a short vowel of one mora length; the sign —— represents a long vowel of two morae length , and the feet are divided by the sign ‖ . The last eight morae must be carried by six syllables only which means that two of them must be long. The first three lines of the 'Riposte' are thus:

```
  ◡‖ —      ◡ ◡   ◡‖ —      ◡ ◡   ◡‖ —    — ◡ ‖ ◡ ◡  —  ◡‖
B a r a a r   h a b a r t i   l o o g   k a m a   f u r t o o ,   g a w r a c   k a m a   b a a j o ,

‖ ◡    ◡ ◡  ◡ ◡ ‖◡ ◡   —   ◡‖ —    — ◡‖ —   ◡ ◡ ◡‖
B i l   s a d d e x   i h i   g a l a b t i i   h a d d a y ,   b e e l o   k a a   b i x i s o ,

‖ ◡ ◡  —   ◡ ‖—   ◡ ◡ ◡ ‖—    — ◡ ‖◡ ◡  —   ◡‖
B e l a d k a a d   u   j e e d d i y o   i f t i i n ,   b e e l o   b a   m a   g e y s o ,
```

The rules of each of the metres are intuitively applied by the poets, who have no explicit knowledge of them but immediately recognize any departures from correctness. No one knows how the system developed but it is certain that it was created without any recourse to writing.

Till the mid 1970s even academic specialists did not know how the system worked; its rules were discovered by two Somali scholars working independently, who published their results in Somali. Their basic discovery was futher developed by John William Johnson at the Folklore Institute at Indiana University, including the discovery of foot boundaries and the relationship between syllables and morae.   Still later Johnson and Alain Barker at the same university found that the verbal meters are far more complex, because they bear a close relationship to additional meters in the music to which they may be sung.

APPENDIX IV

Selected Bibliography

In Somalia surnames are not used and in alphabetical lists it is the given name of a person which appears as the heading of each entry. This system is applied here to Somali names.

1. TRANSLATIONS OF SOMALI POETRY

Andrzejewski, B.W. and I.M. Lewis. *Somali Poetry: An Introduction.* Oxford Library of African Literature. Oxford: Clarendon Press, 1964.

Antinucci, Francesco and Axmed Faarax Cali "Idaajaa". *Poesia orale somala: Storia di una nazione.* Studi Somali 7. Rome: Comitato Tecnico Linguistico per l'Università Nazionale Somala, Ministero degli Affari Esteri, Dipartimento per la Cooperazione allo Sviluppo, 1986.

Axmed Cali Abokor. *The Camel in Somali Oral Traditions.* Trans. Axmed Arten Xange. Uppsala: Somali Academy of Sciences and Arts in cooperation with Scandinavian Institute of African Studies, 1987.

Banti, Giorgio. "La letteratura," in *Aspetti dell'espressione artistica in Somalia: Scrittura e letteratura; strumenti musicali; ornamenti della persona; intaglio del legno,* ed. Annarita Puglielli. Rome: Università di Roma "La Sapienza," 1987, pp.32-71.

Finnegan, Ruth, ed. *The Penguin Book of Oral Poetry.* London: Allen Lane, Penguin Books, 1978. [Contains a number of Somali poems.]

Hassan Sheikh Mumin. *Leopard among the Women - Shabeelnaagood: A Somali Play.* Trans. and ed. by B.W.Andrzejewski. London: Oxford University Press, 1974. [A play in alliterative verse.]

Johnson, John William. *Heellooy, Heelleellooy: The Development of the Genre Heello in Modern Somali Poetry.* Bloomington: Indiana University, 1974.

Laurence, Margaret. *A Tree for Poverty: Somali Poetry and Prose.* Dublin: MacMaster University Library Press and Irish University Press, 1970. First edition: Nairobi, Eagle Press, 1956.

Maxamed Cabdi Maxamed. *Ururin qoraallo la xulay /Receuil de textes choisis.* 2, *Tix /Vers: Chants e poèmes en Somali avec leur traductions.* Besançon: Service Technique de UFR Lettres, 1989.

Yaasiin Cismaan Keenadiid. *Ina Cabdille Xasan e la sua attività letteraria.* Naples: Istituto Universitario Orientale, 1984. [Contains a collection of poems and a general account of Somali oral poetry.]

2. SOMALI POETRY

Andrzejewski, B.W., S.Piłaszewicz and W.Tyloch. *Literatures in African Languages: Theoretical Issues and Sample Surveys.* Cambridge: Cambridge University Press; Warsaw: Wiedza Powszechna, 1985.

Banti, Giorgio. "La letteratura." See Section 1 above.

Loughran, Katheryne S., John L. Loughran, John William Johnson and Said Sheikh Samatar, eds. *Somalia in Word and Image.* Washington, D.C.: Foundation for Cross Cultural Understanding, in cooperation with Indiana University Press, Bloomington, 1986.

Said S.Samatar. *Oral Poetry and Somali Nationalism: The Case of Sayyid Maḥammad Ảbdille Ḥasan.* Cambridge: Cambridge University Press, 1982.

3. ALLITERATION AND SCANSION

Antinucci, Francesco and Axmed Faarax Cali "Idaajaa". *Poesia orale somala: Storia di una nazione.* See Section 1 above.

Görög-Karady, Veronika. *Genres, Forms and Meanings: Essays in African Oral Literature /Genres, Formes, Significations: Essais sur la littérature orale africaine.* Oxford: JASO Occasional Papers, No.1, 1982.

Johnson, John William. "Set Theory in Somali Poetics: Structures and Implications," in *Proceedings of the Third International Congress of Somali Studies*, ed. Annarita Puglielli. Rome: Il Pensiero Scientifico Editore, 1988, pp.123-132.

Maxamed Cabdi Maxamed. *Ururin qoraallo la xulay /Receuil de textes choisis. 2, Tix /Vers Chants e poèmes en Somali avec leur traductions.* See Section 1 above.

4. SOMALI LANGUAGE

Fodor, István and Claude Hagège, eds. *Language Reform: History and Future /La réforme des langues: Histoire et avenir / Sprachreform: Geschichte und Zukunft.* Hamburg: Helmut Buske Verlag, vol.1, 1983. [Contains an account of the introduction of written Somali in 1972.]

Saeed, John Ibrahim. *Somali Reference Grammar.* Wheaton, Maryland: Dunwoody Press, 1987.

5. SOMALI CULTURE AND HISTORY

Abdi Sheikh-Abdi. *Divine Madness: Mohammed Abdulle Hassan (1856-1920).* London and New Jersey: Zed Books, 1992.

Laitin, David D. and Said S.Samatar. *Somalia: Nation in Search of a State.* Boulder, Colorado: Westview Press; London: Gower, 1987.

Lewis, I.M. *A Pastoral Democracy: A Study of Pastoralism and Politics Among the Northern Somali of the Horn of Africa.* London: Oxford University Press for the International African Institute, 1961 Rpt. New York: Africana Publishing Company for the International African Institute, 1982.

Lewis, I.M. *Modern History of Somalia : Nation and State in the Horn of Africa.* Boulder, Colorado: Westview Press; London: Gower Publishing Company and Westview Press, 1988.

6. BIBLIOGRAPHIES

DeLancey, Mark W., Sheila L.Elliott, December Green, Kenneth J. Menk-
haus, Mohammed Haji Moqtar and Peter J.Schräder, compilers.
Somalia. World Bibliographical Series, Vol. 92 Oxford, Santa
Barbara and Denver: Clio Press, 1988. [A general bibliography of
works on Somalia in English.]

Lamberti, Marcello. *Somali Language and Literature.* African Linguistic
Bibliographies 2. Hamburg: Helmut Buske Verlag, 1986.

APPENDIX V

Sources

The original Somali texts of the poem translated in this anthology are found in the sources listed below.

(A) Andrzejewski, B.W. "Modern and Traditional Aspects of Somali Drama," in *Folklore in the Modern World.* Ed. Richard M.Dorson. The Hague and Paris: Mouton Publishers, 1978, pp.87-101.

(B) --------, ed. Somali Poetic Texts: Faarax Cad, "Hadraawi", "Ostreeliya", "Shimbir" and "Yamyam". Typescript. London, 1991.

(C) Axmed Cabdi Haybe. Qamaan Bulxan (Taariikh iyo maanso. Ururintii kowaad). Mogadishu: Akadeemiyaha Cilmiga, Fanka iyo Suugaanta Soomaaliyeed. Typescript, n.d.

(D) Axmed Faarax Cali "Idaajaa". *Ismaaciil Mire.* Mogadishu: Akademiyaha Dhaqaanka, Wasaaradda Hiddaha iyo Tacliinta Sare, 1974.

(E) Caaqib Cabdullaahi Jaamac. Bugga xoog warranka geesigii Wiilwaal iyo taariikhdiisa iyo umuuro kale oo raacsan. Mogadishu: Akademiyada Cilmiga, Fanka iyo Suugaanta. Typescript, 1977. [Note that "Bugga xoog warranka" would normally be written "Buugga xog warranka" in Somali orthography.]

(F) Hassan Sheikh Mumin. *Leopard among the Women - Shabeelnaagood: A Somali Play.* Trans. and ed. by B.W.Andrzejewski. London: School of Oriental and African Studies, Oxford University Press, 1974.

(G) Jaamac Cumar Ciise, Sheekh, ed. *Diiwaanka gabayadii Sayid Maxamad Cabdulle Xasan.* Mogadishu: Akademiyaha Dhaqanka, Wasaaradda Hiddaha iyo Tacliinta Sare, 1974.

(H) ---------, Aw, ed. *Taariikhdii Daraawiishta iyo Sayid Cabdulle Xasan 1895-1921).* Mogadishu: Akadeemiyaha Dhaqanka, Wasaaradda Hiddaha iyo Tacliinta Sare, 1976.

(I) Mohamed Farah Abdillahi. Noloshii Cilmi Bowndheri. Typescript. London, 1965.

(J) Muuse Ḥaaji Ismaa'iil Galaal. *Hikmad Soomaali* . Edited by B.W. Andrzejewski. London: Oxford University Press, 1956.

(K) Rashiid Maxamed Shabeele. *Ma dhabba jacayl waa loo dhintaa?* Mogadishu: Wakaaladda Madbacaddaa Qaranka, 1975.

(L) Shire Jaamac Achmed. *Gabayo, maahmaah iyo sheekooyin yaryar* Mogadishu: The National Printers, 1965.

(M) Wasaaradda Waxbarashada iyo Barbaarinta, Xafiiska Manaahijta. *Suugaan. Fasalka Koowaad, Dugsiyada Sare.* Mogadishu, 1976.

(N) --------. *Suugaan. Fasalka Labaad, Dugsiyada Sare.* Mogadishu, 1977.

(O) --------. *Buugga Suugaanta. Fasalka Saddexaad, Dugsiga Sare.* Mogadishu, 1978.

(P) --------. *Buugga Suugaanta. Fasalka Afraad, Dugsiga Sare.* Mogadishu, n.d.

(Q) Yaasiin Cismaan Keenadiid. *Ina Cabdille Xasan e la sua attività letteraria.* Naples: Istituto Universitario Orientale, 1984.

(R) Yusuuf Meygaag Samatar. *Madhaafaanka murtida.* Mogadishu: Madbaacadda Dawladda, 1973. [Note that "Yusuuf" would normally be written "Yuusuf" in Somali orthography.]

Typescripts (B), (C), (E) and (I) have been deposited with the library of the School of Oriental and African Studies, University of London, and in that of Indiana University.

The precise location of the originals is shown by means of groups of figures and capital letters. The figures which precede the letters are serial numbers of the poems as given in the Contents, while the letters refer to the sources listed above. Figures after the letters are page references.

1 (Q) 102-103; 2 (L) 32 (Lines 1-16); 3 (R) 13-14;

4 (L) 31-32 (Lines 4-18); **5** (L) 46 (Lines 1-10); **6** (E) 10;

7 (N) 31-34; **8** (N) 6-7; **9** (B) 2;

1 0 (M) 45-46; **11** (M) 22-23; **12** (G) 295-299;

1 3 (G) 137-138; **14** (G) 142-145; **15** (G) 58-62 (Lines 1-30 & 34-99);

16 (G) 93; **17** (G) 158-162; **18** (G) 286;

19 (H) 309; **20** (D) 41; **21** (D) 156-158;

2 2 (D) 152-154; **23** (D) 133-135 (Lines 3-31); **24** (D) 121-122;

25 (O) 37-38; **26** (O) 51; **27** (C) 34-36;

2 8 (M) 10; **29** (I) 6; **30** (K) 67;

31 (I) 5-6; **32** (L) 41-42; **33** (N) 12-14 (Lines 1-62 & 73-86);

3 4 (B) 15-16; **35** (J) 53, 56-57, 59-61; **36** (B) 20;

3 7 (A) 89; **38** (F) 110-112; **39** (P) 39-40;

40 (K) 11-12, 14-15; **41** (P) 56-58.

B. W. ANDRZEJEWSKI is Emeritus Professor of Cushitic Languages and Literatures in the University of London, where he was a faculty member in the School of Oriental and African Studies from 1952 to 1982.

SHEILA ANDRZEJEWSKI (née Weekes) accompanied her husband on most of his research travels and shares his interest in the literary culture of Somalia.

Lightning Source UK Ltd.
Milton Keynes UK
UKOW04f2115201214

243412UK00001B/38/P